ANCIENT CURES, CHARMS, AND USAGES OF IRELAND

CONTRIBUTIONS TO IRISH LORE

First Edition 1890
Lady Wilde

New Edition 2019
Edited by Tarl Warwick

COPYRIGHT AND DISCLAIMER

FOREWORD

"Ancient Cures, Charms, and Usages of Ireland" is quite an interesting work, penned at the end of the 19th century, an era of significant upheaval within all European theaters. It is split into sections, loosely defined, covering many sub-topics.

First comes the medicinal- simple healing charmes and a few herbal recipes for various complaints, mostly topical in nature. Much of the lore here is straightly Catholic in derivation and involves prayer as much as healing botanically.

Second there are some (mostly spooky) folk tales, often involving individuals being carried off by the Devil or otherwise bewitched for their malevolent behavior or else tricked in romance and marriage by some means. Many of the stories it presents involve an apparent distrust of females- at least as analyzed retrospectively. A large number of these works additionally involve fairies- which here are regarded specifically as being concerned with carrying off children or, on occasion, bewitching young males in order to seduce and marry them. A few of the works are more chilling and involve a weird sort of fascination with romancing the deceased.

The third section of this work deals with Irish history and politics and advocates nothing less than the invasion of the island by Americans in order to liberate the people there from perpetual tyranny- a step now vestigial but then considered seriously by some. It is both exceptionally pro-Irish and universally in acclamation of the United States.

The final (and shortest) section is a collection of simple proverbs- short statements of wisdom, which generally applaud hard work and caution and dissuade excess and undue optimism.

ANCIENT CURES, CHARMS, AND USAGES OF IRELAND

Altogether the work is fairly comprehensive. It contains an explicitly civic bent in addition to the folklore itself. This is amusing now, more than a century later, since Ireland has full independence and its former task master has declined into a lesser power as Englands' dominions, one by one, revolted and eventually gained freedom; often for the better, occasionally for the worse.

This edition of "Ancient Cures, Charms, and Usages of Ireland" has been carefully edited for grammar and format. Care has been taken to retain all original intent and meaning.

ANCIENT CURES, CHARMS, AND USAGES OF IRELAND

THE EARLY RACES

All nations and races from the earliest time have held the intuitive belief that mystic beings were always around them, influencing, though unseen, every action of life, and all the forces of nature. They felt the presence of a spirit in the winds, and the waves, and the swaying branches of the forest trees, and in the primal elements of all that exists. Fire was to them the sacred symbol of the divine essence, ever striving towards ascension; and water, ever seeking a level, was the emblem of the purification that should cover all daily life; while in the elemental earth they reverenced the power that produces all things, and where all that lives finds a grave, yet also a resurrection.

Thus to the primitive races of mankind the unseen world of mystery was a vital and vivid reality; the great over-soul of the visible, holding a mystic and psychic relation to humanity, and ruling it through the instrumentality of beings who had a strange power either for good or evil over human lives and actions. We turn back the leaves of the national legends of all countries and peoples, and find stamped on the first page the words 'God and Immortality.' These two ideas are at the base of all the old-world thought and culture, and underlie all myths, rituals, and monuments, and all the antique usages and mystic lore of charms, incantations, and sacrificial observances.

The primal idea may be often degraded, debased, and obscured by the low instincts of , savage man; yet, religious faith is the basis of all superstitions, and in all of them can be traced the ceaseless and instinctive effort of humanity to incarnate and make manifest this prescience within the soul of the unseen dominating the seen, with the desire, also, to master the forces of nature through the aid of these invisible spirits. It is worthy of note, also, that the mythology and superstitions of a people are far more faithful guides as to the origin and affinity of races than language, which, through commerce and conquest, is perpetually changing, till the ancient idiom is at last crushed out and lost by the dominance of the stronger and conquering nation.

But the myths, superstitions, and legends (which are the expression of a people's faith), remain fixed and fast through successive generations, and finally become so inwoven with the daily life of the people that they form part of the national character and cannot be dissevered from it. This is especially true of the Irish, who, having been wholly separated from European thought and culture for countless centuries, by their language and insular position at the extreme limit of the known world, have remained unchanged in temperament and nature; still clinging to the old traditions with a fervor and faith that would make them, even now, suffer death sooner than violate a superstition, or neglect those ancient usages of their fathers which have held them in bonds since the first dawn of history. For the customs and usages of the Irish race can be traced far back, even to the Egyptian and Pelasgian influence that dominated the primal tribes of humanity, ever wandering westward by the shores and islands of the great sea. The Celtic tribes followed the earlier Pelasgian along the same line of westward migration, carrying with them Egyptian and Pelasgian ideas even beyond the Pillars of Hercules, till they reached the shores of the distant Hibernia, where pre-historic monuments, supposed to be of Pelasgian origin, are still existing to attest the presence of that ancient people- such as the grand and wonderful Temple of New Grange, at the Boyne, one of those eternal works of the hand of man over which time seems to have no power.

ANCIENT CURES, CHARMS, AND USAGES OF IRELAND

Irish customs also resemble the Hebrew in many things; for all nations have preserved fragments of the one primal creed, and have many elements in common as regards religious beliefs and ritual. The Jews borrowed from Egypt, as the Egyptians borrowed from Babylon and Chaldea. Thus the creeds, symbols, and usages of all the early nations have a certain basis of identity.

The Irish, however, have retained more of the ancient superstitions than any other European people, and hold to them with a reverential belief that cannot be shaken by any amount of modern philosophic teaching. They are also, perhaps, indebted to Egypt for the wonderful knowledge of the power of herbs, which has always characterized the Irish, both among the adepts and the peasants.

THE IRISH DOCTORS

From the most ancient pagan times, the Irish doctors were renowned for their skill in the treatment of disease, and the professors of medicine held a high and influential position in the Druid order. They were allowed a distinguished place at the royal table, next to the nobles, and above the armorers, smiths, and workers in metals; they were also entitled to wear a special robe of honor when at the courts of the kings, and were always attended by a large staff of pupils, who assisted the master in the diagnosis and treatment of disease, and the preparations necessary for the curative potions.

The skill of the Irish physicians was based chiefly upon a profound knowledge of the healing nature and properties of herbs; and they were also well acquainted with the most deadly and concentrated poisons that can be found in the common field plants. But, in addition to the aid given by science and observation, they also practiced magic with great effect, knowing well how strongly charms, incantations, and fairy cures can act on the nerves and impress the mind of a patient. Consequently their treatment of disease was of a medico-religious character, in which various magic ceremonials largely helped the curative process.

THE TUATHA DE DANAN

The oldest record of physicians in Ireland dates from the battle of Magh-tura (Moytura, the plain of the Towers) fought about three thousand years ago between the Firbolgs, the primitive, unlettered dwellers in Erin, and the Tuatha-de-Danans, a new set of invaders from the Isles of the Sea, more learned and powerful than the Firbolgs, skilled as metal workers, and famous as warriors and physicians.

At this great historic battle of Moytura, Dianecht, the chief physician of the Tuatha, had a bath of herbs prepared, at the rear of the army, of singular efficacy, into which the wounded were plunged, and from which they emerged healed and whole. During the fierce combat, Nuada, the King of the Tuatha, lost his hand; but it is recorded that Dianecht made for him a silver hand, fashioned with the most perfect mechanical and artistic skill; and henceforth the King was known as Nuada Airgeat-lamh (Nuad of the silver hand), and by this name he lives in history. Owing to their great knowledge and skill in metallurgy, the Firbolgs looked on the powerful invaders as necromancers and enchanters, and fled before them to the extreme limit of the western coast, even out to the remote Arran Isles, where they built, for shelter and protection from the enemy, those marvelous Cyclopean forts, whose stupendous, ruins, with the causeway leading to them, formed of enormous masses of stone, can be seen to this day. After this, until the final conquest of Ireland by the Milesians from Spain, the Tuatha long remained masters of Ireland, and learning and art flourished under their rule. An ancient poet thus describes their great medical power:

> "The Tuatha by force of potent spells,
> Could raise a slaughtered army from the earth,
> And make them live, and breathe, and fight again."

Adjoining the royal palace or 'Tara of the Kings' they erected a hospital called 'The House of Sorrow' where the wounded knights and chiefs were carried after the battles and forays to be healed of their wounds, and were attended there by the doctor and his staff of pupils until quite restored. But if the liaigh, or leech, took up his abode at the house of the patient, he was entitled to his diet, along with four of his pupils, in addition to his fees, during the healing of the wound. If the cure, however, did not make satisfactory progress, the liaigh was obliged to pay for the food already consumed, and to refund the fees, which were handed over to a better liaigh.

ANCIENT DOCTORS OF IRELAND

The practice of physic was hereditary in certain families, and each of the nobles had a special physician attached to his service. In the more ancient times, medical knowledge was handed down by oral tradition from father to son; then, as learning advanced, by written books, carefully preserved in each family. The sons were generally educated by their fathers in the practice of physic, but it is said that Dianecht, being jealous of the superior skill of his son, caused him to be slain, when from the grave of the youth sprang a number of herbs, all efficacious in curing disease; and thus, though dead, he carried on his work.

After the introduction of Christianity by St. Patrick, schools were established both for law; and physic, where Latin was sedulously taught and freely spoken. Camden describes these schools, and says of them: "They speak Latin there like the

ANCIENT CURES, CHARMS, AND USAGES OF IRELAND

vulgar tongue, conning by rote the aphorisms of Hippocrates, Galen, Avicenna, and others among the great masters of surgery."

ANCIENT MEDICAL MANUSCRIPTS

Numerous copies of these ancient writers were made by the learned doctors and freely distributed among the profession, so that many of the manuscripts can still be found in the chief libraries of Europe. They are written on vellum, and are beautiful specimens of penmanship. A commentary in Irish was sometimes added, besides which, several translations into Irish of the chief medical works whole and entire, are in existence.

In proof of the great and accurate knowledge of these Irish physicians, it is stated by Sir William Wilde, that when preparing "The Status of Diseased from the Earliest Times," for the Irish census, he was able to tabulate seventy-five fatal diseases accurately described by the native doctors, with many that were not fatal; and he asserts that the Irish terms for the principal diseases were of far more appropriate significance than those at present employed in English, or derived from the Latin and Greek.

DRUIDIC CHARMS

Meantime, the ancient Druidic charms and invocations continued to hold their power over the people, who believed in them with undoubting faith. No doubt, in pagan times, the invocations were made in the names of Baal and Ashtaroth, and by the power of the sun, the moon, and the winds; but the Christian converts, while still retaining the form of the ancient charms, substituted the names of the Trinity and the words of the Christian Ritual as still more powerful in effecting cures. And in this mode they are used to the present day among the peasants, who consider them as talismans of magic power when said over the sick; and no amount of argument would shake their faith in these mystic formulas which have some down to them through centuries of tradition; nor would any one venture to laugh at them, or an evil fate would certainly fall on the scorner. For, above all things, fervent faith is necessary while the mystic words are uttered, or the charm will not work for good; and charms were set with most effect upon Wednesdays and Fridays, and must be set fasting, generally before sunrise.

ANCIENT CHARMS

A few examples of these ancient cures and charms may be given to show their simple, half-religious character, so well calculated to impress a. people like the Irish, of intense faith and a strong instinct for the mystic and the supernatural. (I have already included many ancient Irish charms
in my published work, entitled " Ancient Legends of|
Ireland," to which I must refer the reader who may bei
interested in the subject.)

For the Falling Sickness

"By the wood of the Cross, by the Man that overcame death, be thou healed." These words are to be said in the left ear while the fit is on the patient, and he is to be signed three times with the sign of the Cross, in. the name of God and the blessed Lord, when by virtue of the charm he will be cured.

A Charm against Accidents, Fire, Tempests, Water, Knife, or Lance

"Jesus, Saviour of men. In Jesus trust, and in Mary trust truly for all grace." This is the measure of the wounds of Christ upon the Cross, which was brought to Constants nople to the Emperor as a most precious relic, so that no evil enemy might have power over him.

And whoever reads it, or tears it, cannot be hurt by fire or tempest, or the knife, or the lance; neither can the devil have power over him, nor will he die an untimely death, but safety from all dangers will be his to the end."

For a Sprain

As St. Agnes went over the moor to the mountain of Moses, she fell with her foot turned. But sinew to sinew, and bone to bone, God makes all right to him who has faith: and be thou healed, O man, in Jesus' name. Amen.

For the Ague

When Christ first saw the cross on which He was to be crucified, He trembled very exceedingly. And the Jews asked Him, "Hast Thou the fever, or the ague?", "No," He answered, "neither of these do I fear, for God is above all." Wherefore, when the fit comes on, let the person afflicted repeat these words of Christ, and be will be calmed.

For a Wound that Bleeds

"A child was baptized in the river Jordan; and the water was dark and muddy, but the child was pure and beautiful." Say these words over the wound, placing the finger on the spot where the blood flows, adding: "In the name of God and of the Lord Christ, let the blood be staunched." And if the patient have faith, so shallwill be.

For Toothache

Drink water from a human skull; or take a pinch of clay

from a priest's grave, and put it in your mouth. Then kneel down, say a Pater and an Ave, and you will have no more toothache as long as you live.

A Cure for Weakness

Drink of the water of a river forming the boundary of three properties for nine Sunday mornings, before sunrise, fasting, and before any one has crossed the stream. In silence it must be done, and without speaking to anyone; but afterwards repeat nine Aves and the Credo.

For Consumption

The Crow-Darrig, or Red Hand, to be pulled, by tying it to a cock's leg, or the leg of a dog otherwise it is fatal to the one who pulls it. The leaves to be squeezed, and the juice taken, fasting, every Wednesday morning. The leaves then to be carefully burned.

For Inflammation

Nine handfuls of mountain moss, dried on a pan to powder. Nine pinches of it, and nine pinches of the ashes from the hearth, to be mixed in whey, taken every Tuesday and Thursday.

For Whooping Cough

Put a live trout into the child's mouth, fasting. Then put it back alive into the stream. If a trout cannot be had, a frog may be tried. The tooth of a dead horse or the hand of a dead man rubbed over the jaw, will also be found effective to ease the pain of an ailing tooth.

ANCIENT CURES

For Cramp

An eel's skin tied round the knee alleviates pain, and for deafness nothing is esteemed better than constant anointing with the oil of eels, used perfectly fresh.

For the Nine-day Fever

Write the name of Jesus nine times on a slip of paper, then cut the paper into small bits, mix the pieces with some soft food, and make the patient swallow it. So will he be cured if he trusts in the Lord.

For Mumps

Tie a halter round the child's neck, then lead it to a brook and bathe him, dipping him three times in the name of the Trinity.

CHARMS AND CURES

For a Sprain

A young girl, under fourteen years of age, spins a thread dry, that is, without using saliva; then she ties it round the leg or the arm afflicted, and when the cure is completed the thread miraculously disappears. Chickweed is also used as a poultice. Galen notices the virtue of this herb, and extols its use to remove stiffness or swellings.

ANCIENT CURES, CHARMS, AND USAGES OF IRELAND

For Rickets

A blacksmith, whose fathers have been smiths for three generations, must carry the child in his apron three times round the anvil for seven days in succession, repeating the Paternoster each time, but no money must be accepted for the cure.

For Epilepsy

Cut a twig of elder tree into nine parts, and string the pieces as a necklace to be tied round the patient's neck; but should the necklace fall and touch the ground, it must be burned, and a new one made.

For the Staunching of Blood

"There came a man from Bethlehem to be baptized in the river Jordan; but the water was so muddy that it stopped flowing. So let the blood! So let the blood! Let it stop flowing in the name of Jesus, and by the power of Christ!" This is said in a loud voice over the patient, while a scarlet worsted is tied tightly round the wrists and round the throat, to stop the course of the blood.

For a Burn

A lone widow-woman from the Antrim shore, who had the gift of second-sight and the knowledge of many charms, used the following to cure a burn; Lay your right hand very softly over the burn, then repeat these words three times over unto yourself, giving a gentle blast each time from your mouth on the place burned:

"Old clod beneath the clay,
Burn away, burn away.

In the name of God be thou healed. Amen."

After this the pain will cease, and a deep sleep will fall on the patient.

Another Charm foe Burns

Blow upon the burn three times, repeating the words:

"Two angels sat upon a stone,
One was Fire, the other Frost,
Praise Father, Son, and Holy Ghost."

It is believed in the South and West, that if a person is licked by the lizard called the 'Mankeeper,' he will never suffer from burns, and can even heal them in another by his touch; for a man one day having trod on a lizard found that he had acquired this power by the contact. In modern times a plaster of potatoes, scraped as for starch, is constantly applied for a burn, and gives great ease. Fried cabbage-leaves are also used by the people to deaden the pain; but a plant of house-leek affixed to the thatch of the roof should not be forgotten, as this preserves the inmates of the cabin from scalds, burns, and the danger of fire as long as it remains untouched.

For Whooping Cough

Take a mug of water from a running stream, against the current; give the child a drink, then throw the rest away with the current; repeat this for three mornings before sunrise, and the cure will be perfected.

For a Mote in the Eye

An incantation is to be said by a fairy-woman over a

plate of water. Then the patient is to look steadily at the plate, and the mote will drop into the water, and the eye become clear. The most powerful charm against ill-luck is a horse-shoe made red-hot, then tied up at the entrance door, and never after touched or taken down.

For Contusions

Heat a great stone in the fire, and, when red hot, throw it into water, and bathe the bruise with the liquid. Repeat this treatment twice a day, always first heating the stone, and the cure is certain in a few days.

For the Bite of a Mad Dog

A charm which Columkill applied to a wound, brimful of poison, and it took away the venom:

"Arise, Cormac O'Clunan, through Christ be thou healed. By the hand of Christ be thou healed, in blood, marrow, and bone, and may the poison die in thee as I sign the sign of the Cross."

This oration to be said over the person bitten, while butter is given him to eat. It may also be said over a cow or a horse, but never over a hog or dog.

For Suspected Witchcraft

The forge dust of three different forges, well mixed together, to be given to the patient while Paters and Aves are recited; or the herb called Lusmore may be used as very effectual against witchcraft. It is a powerful poison, and the patient is rubbed all over with it, though the practice is dangerous, as the bewitched person may die under the treatment, especially if tied naked to a stake, as was the custom in old times, while the imprecation is said: "If you are bewitched, or fairy-struck, may the devil take you away, with the curse on your head for ever and ever."

For Jaundice

Elder ointment is of great repute; also a salad made of various herbs by the wise women, called the green ointment, is considered a sovereign remedy.

All the ancient cures were derived from the animal and the vegetable world, never from the mineral kingdom. A very ancient belief pervaded the South and West, that twelve large earth-worms baked upon a shovel, then reduced to powder, and made into a philter to be drank every morning, was an unfailing remedy for jaundice, but not long since the child of a gentleman of rank in the West was nearly poisoned by a dose of this physic, for the nurse, being dissatisfied with the treatment of the doctor in attendance, secretly gave a drink of the philter to the little patient, who so nearly died of it that the nurse was tried for an attempt to murder.

The Homoeopathic adepts among the Irish doctors always employ yellow medicines for the jaundice, as saffron, turmeric, sulfur, and even yellow soap. The Allopaths employ other remedies, especially the leaves of the barbary tree, which is held to be a specific, if brewed to a strong drink, and taken every morning, fasting, for nine days in succession. An adept in the County Galway attracted great crowds to his dwelling recently by his wonderful cures for jaundice and other diseases. The remedy used was simply a dose of tartar emetic, administered freely for every form of ailment, and often the result was most satisfactory.

The fairy-doctors use the following cure:

Nine young shoots from the root of an ash tree that had been cut down. These are placed in a bottle, which is then buried in a secluded spot, the patient not being allowed to see it. As long as the bottle remains in the ground, he is safe from the disease; but, should it be broken, he will have a relapse and probably die from mental emotion, caused by fear of the result, before many days are over.

For Sore Eyes

The most efficacious treatment for diseases of the eye is a pilgrimage to a holy well, for the blessed waters have a healing power for all ophthalmic ailments, and can even give sight to the blind. Pearls upon the eye are said to be removed by an amber bead, the tenth upon the rosary, rubbed upon the eye; and the wise woman of the village will show the amber bead, with a white substance adhering, which she affirms is the pearl removed by the mystic attraction of the amber. Also the shell of a living snail is pierced with a pin, and the fluid that exudes is used as healing for the eyes. This cure is called the 'Snail Drop.' Severe counter-irritation upon the crown of the head has been long used by the wise women, and with wonderful success. The crown of the head is first shaved, and then a plaster is applied, made of coarse lint and white of egg spread upon a piece of tow. This is left on till a blister rises, when the cure speedily follows. This remedy of counter-irritation is, however, now well known and recognized by the medical profession, and largely used in ophthalmic surgery.

Fasting spittle is considered of great efficacy by the peasants for sore eyes, especially if mixed with clay taken from a holy well. This is made into a paste and applied to the eyes, and the people say 'nothing beats the fasting spittle for blessedness.'

ANCIENT CURES, CHARMS, AND USAGES OF IRELAND

To avert the evil eye from child or beast, it is necessary to spit upon it on entering a cabin; and if a stranger looks fixedly and admiringly on a child, he is at once requested to spit upon it; this saving process being perhaps unknown to him or if he should not understand Irish, and omit the rite that preserves from evil, then the old mother will rise up from her seat by the fire and perform the ceremony herself, that so good luck may not depart from the house.

CHARMS AND CURES

For Dyspepsia

Fix a small piece of candle on a penny piece, then lay the patient on his back and place the penny on the region of the stomach; light the candle, and over all place a well-dried tumbler, when the skin will be drawn up, as in cupping. This is called 'the lifting of the evil from the body.' For epilepsy there are many cures, but chiefly by exorcism. When the priest is called upon to exorcise the evil spirit, he puts on his sacred garments for the ceremony, sprinkles the patient with holy water, and recites prayers over him till the fit leaves him. If, however, this treatment does not succeed, the priest will not repeat the exorcism, saying: "Leave him to God. The will of the Lord must be done." Another cure is also used: A harrow-pin, a piece of money, and cuttings of the hair and nails of the patient are buried deep down in the earth, on the spot where lie fell in the fit, and he is given a drink of holy water, in which nine hairs from the tail of a black cat have been steeped.

For Asthma

Let the patient drink of a potion made of dandelion (dent-de-lion - lion's tooth) or of ground ivy, made and used in the same way, with prayer said over it before drinking.

The red rash is cured by applying unsalted butter to the part affected, while the Ave Maria is said. Also the blood of a hare is very efficacious if applied to the skin with a red rag, and the rag afterwards buried.

For whooping cough, a lock of hair, cut from the head of a person who never saw his father, is to be tied up in a piece of red cloth and worn round the neck.

Dropsy

This disorder was not prevalent in Ireland in early times, but since the general use of potatoes as diet among the villagers, along with the copious amount of whiskey drank in the towns, the disease has become very common.

Fasting Spittle

In former times spittle was used in baptism, and in many of the daily transactions of life, as a lucky and confirmatory act; and even now no bargain is concluded at fair or market till the receiver lays the money in the palm of his hand and spits upon it. The head of the faction fight likewise spits upon his blackthorn stick to make the blow more deadly and certain. But, for a perfect result, the saliva should be used fasting, especially after a black fast, when the person had not even tasted water. It is also effectual as a cure for chapped lips when mixed with dust and applied in the name of the Trinity.

For the Night Fever

Take a ribbon and tie it tightly round the head of the sick person, saying: "In the name of Father, Son, and Holy Ghost, let the fever go from thy head, man, and be thou healed."

ANCIENT CURES

If a cow becomes restive, plunges about, or lies down with her nose to the ground, she is said to have the feist, or worm. To cure this, a long string is taken and twisted into a knot, like a coiled worm; and the curious knot seems so firmly knitted that it never could be untied. Yet there is a mode of drawing out the two ends, when the coil disappears and the string is quite free. This is done three times while the Paternoster is said over the animal, when the most beneficial result is sure to follow. This cure is called snaidhen-na-peista (the worm's knot), and is of great antiquity.

For the King's Evil

There are certain wise men among the peasants who keep pieces of paper, transmitted from their fathers, which, they say, have been steeped in a king's blood. And if the paper is rubbed over the patient in the name of the Trinity, he will be cured.

For Rheumatism

The bone of the haddock that lies under the mark of Christ's fingers is always to be carried in the pocket. This bone has many other virtues, and always works good to the owner; but it must not be exhibited, and it should never be lent, or touched except by the owner.

To Remove Warts

Tie up some pebbles in a bag with a piece of silver money, and throw it on the road; whoever finds the bag and keeps the money, to him the warts will go, and leave you forever.

Also, steal a piece of meat and apply it raw to the warts; then, bury it in the ground, and as the meat decays the warts will disappear. Bat the charm is of no use unless the meat is stolen, and no one should see you either stealing or burying it. For other ailments there are many curious usages employed by the people that have come down by tradition, and in which they have the greatest faith, and the faith, perhaps, effects the cure.

For the slaedan, or influenza, some clay must be scraped off the threshold, made into a paste and applied as a plaster to the chest. But, to be effective, the clay must be taken from the very spot where a person first sets his foot on entering the house, when it is the custom to say, "God save all here," for these numerous blessings have given the clay a peculiar power to cure the chest and help the voice when it is affected, But the holy power is only for him who believes, for by his faith he will be made whole.

For a Sty

The tail of a black cat, if rubbed over the eye, will effect a speedy cure. It is good, also, to point nine thorns in succession at the eye, without touching it, throwing away each one after use over the left shoulder.

CHARMS AND CURES

For a Headache

Measuring the head for nervous headache is much practiced. The measuring doctor has certain days for practicing his art, and receives or visits his patients on no other occasions. He first measures the head with a piece of tape above the ears and across the forehead, then from ear to ear over the crown of the head, then diagonally across the vertex. After this he uses strong compression with his hands, and declares that the head is 'too open' And he mutters certain prayers and charms at the same time. This process is repeated for three days, until at last the doctor asserts that the head is closing and has grown much smaller- in proof he shows his measurements; and the cure is completed when he pronounces the head to be 'quite closed,' on which the headache immediately vanishes, and the patient is never troubled by it again.

ANCIENT CURES

They say in Shark Island, that any man who rubs his tongue over a lizard's back will be given power to cure a burn by applying the tongue to the part affected.

Some wool taken, from a black sheep, and worn, constantly in the ear, is a sure remedy for earache.

Spiders are of great use in curing disease. A few tied up in a bag, and worn round the neck, will keep off fever and ague; but none, save the fairy doctor, must ever open the bag to look at the contents, or the charm would be broken. Also a black spider, laid as a sandwich between two slices of bread-and-butter, and eaten- one every morning- will be found a great strengthener of the body.

The king's evil is cured by the blood of a black cat. A peasant woman had a cat whose tail was almost entirely nipped off by the repeated applications made for a drop of the creature's blood. Finally the cat was carried away altogether, probably to effect a speedy cure by the more copious use of poor pussy's healing blood.

POPULAR CURES

Spiders are used for many ailments, especially for ague. A small living spider should be rolled up in a cobweb, then put into a lump of butter and eaten while the fit is on. Pills, also, may be made of the cobwebs in which the eggs remain, and taken daily for three days; after which time it would be dangerous to continue the treatment. The spider's web is also an excellent styptic, and is still in use among all classes for the staunching of blood, or any abrasion of the skin.

In the operation of bleeding, salt was first sprinkled on the plate and in the cup, and the lips of the patient were touched with the first drops of blood that flowed. It is considered unlucky to bleed a young girl in the arm; the operator therefore, when possible, bleeds her in the foot, which is first placed for some time in warm water.

Duckweed boiled down, and the liquid drank three times a day, is an excellent potion for the sick.

The Falling Sickness

Burn the patient with a red-hot church key along the head, and he will be cured. Should he fall in the fit, put the juice of absinthe, or fennel juice, or sage juice into his mouth, and he will get well at once.

For Sore Eyes (1460)

A charge of great power, called 'The Charge of the Artificer's Son,' and from the Danes it was got; and these are the herbs: onions and dillisk, with ambrosia and garlic; and let the plants be broken and boiled upon beer; then add the gall of a hog's liver and a drop of wine or of doe's milk, and, when well strained, pour it into an amphora of brass, and apply the liquid to the eye, when the benefit is certain.

Another illustrious charge is made of white lily, valerian, and the leaves of the rowan tree. Also yarrow, and honey, and the gall of fish boiled together and strained, then applied to the eye, will carry off every description of blindness and clear the pains of the head.

Mesmerism

Charms, relics, holy wells, stroking by an adept, and the hand of a seventh son, are all esteemed infallible curative agents. But the seventh son born in succession, without a daughter intervening, has the power of curing pains and aches by merely waving his hand over the part affected. He must, however, first pray in silence for power and strength. Mesmerism has been practiced in Ireland from Druidic times, and cures were effected by waving of the hands without contact, or by stroking. The phenomenon of clairvoyance, called in Irish the 'enlightenment,' was also well known to the Druids, who by this means ascertained the will of the gods in important matters, and by its aid prophecies were made and the thoughts of the heart revealed. Rheumatism was chiefly cured by stroking, and all remedies that acted on the imagination, such as lying in a saint's bed, mesmeric charms, and incantations, were deemed most effectual. Latin words were used as charms, sewn up in a bag and carried in the pocket, tied round the hind legs of a hare. An eel-skin had great virtue placed on the chest, or tied round the knee. Forge water had many virtues and could allay rheumatic pains; also potato water, used hot, with the froth on.

ANCIENT CURES, CHARMS, AND USAGES OF IRELAND

Erysipelas

Called by the Irish the 'wild fire,' is believed to originate from fairy malice; and blood must be spilled to cure the disease. The blood of a black cat is best, consequently few of these animals can be seen with an entire tail, for it is nipped off bit by bit to perform the cure. The black cat is a very weird and mysterious creature. If you manage to possess one particular bone of it, you can at will render yourself invisible. To obtain this, boil the cat alive, then take the bones one by one, and hold each singly in your mouth before a looking-glass, strictly observing if the bone is reflected there; for should you happen to hold one in your mouth that is not reflected, then you may know that the mystic bone at last is found which will make you invisible at pleasure.

If a cow is sick, the witch-man or charmer mounts astride on the animal, and is given a bannock to eat, well buttered, along with a bowl of cream; these he takes, saying: "A bite, a sup, a bite, a sup; if it be so ordained, let the beast get well; if not, leave it to its fate; but the bannock I will eat."

A wise woman, learned in the mysteries, has been known to cure the depression of spirits, called in Irish 'the sinking of the heart,' in the following manner. Holding a cup of meal close to the patient, the operator says in Irish: "Base to the heart, ease to the heart," at the same time repeating the words of an invocation known only to herself, and which has never been written down. This is done on Monday, Thursday, and the Monday following, each time the meal being cast into the fire after use. Then a cake is made of the remainder, the patient sitting by till it is baked, taking care that neither cat, nor dog, nor any living thing passes between him and the fire till the cake is baked and the sign of the Cross made over it. It is then eaten with nine sprigs of watercress, and if any is left, it must be thrown into the fire, so that no animal should touch it, the sign of the blessed Cross being stamped thereon.

The peasants have such faith in the ancient cures that, in case of accident or sickness, they would far sooner trust the wise woman of the village than all the dispensary doctors in Ireland. One of these authorized practitioners narrates that a woman once consulted him about a severe affection of the throat, and when examining her he found that she had a scarlet worsted thread tied round the throat, and another round the wrists. Asking the meaning of this, she said that the old wise woman of the place had given them to her the night before as a certain cure. "So, as they did no harm," added the doctor, "I left them on, though meanwhile I added what I considered best, and under the usual medical treatment she soon became quite well. But, all the same, she believed in the scarlet thread, and secretly thought that by its power she was cured of her ailment."

Love Charms

Philters, love powders, and charms to procure affection were frequently used in Ireland, and the belief in them existed from the most ancient times. The bardic legends have frequent allusions to love charms; but the most awful of all is the dead strip. Girls have been known to go to a graveyard at night, exhume a corpse that had been nine days buried, and tear down a strip of the skin from head to foot; this they manage to tie round the leg or arm of the man they love while he sleeps, taking care to remove it before his awaking. And so long as the girl keeps this strip of skin in her possession, secretly hidden from all eyes, so long will she retain the man's love.

Madness

There was a terrible care employed in old times for insanity, which the people believed in with implicit faith. It consisted in burying the patient for three days and three nights in the earth. A pit was dug, three feet wide and six feet deep, in which the patient was placed, only the head being left uncovered; and during the time of the care he was allowed no food, and no one was permitted to speak to him, or even to approach him. A harrow-pin was placed over his body, for the harrow-pin is supposed to have peculiar mystic attributes, and was always used in ancient sorceries, and then the unhappy patient was left alone. If he survived the living burial, he was generally taken out of the pit more dead than alive, perished with cold and hunger, and more mad than ever. Yet it was averred that sometimes the senses were actually restored by this inhuman treatment.

The Falling Sickness

This sickness is best cured by the hand of a priest. But it is said that if on the first attack the person's shirt be taken off and thrown into the fire and burned, his hair cropped, and his nails pared, and the hair and the parings buried, together with a young cock put down into the grave alive, then lie will never have another attack while he lives.

Madness is also cured by giving the person three substances not procured by human means, and not made by the hand of man. These are honey, milk, and salt, and they are to be given him to drink before sunrise in a sea-shell. Madness and the falling sickness are both considered hereditary, and caused by demoniacal possession.

For king's evil, a most effective cure of proved power is made of burdock roots, the common dock, bog-bean, and rose-noble boiled in water, of which the patient must drink three times a day.

Vervain and the mountain ash are the best preservatives for cattle against witchcraft. Some should be tied round the cow's horns and her tail. Then no fairy or witch can do harm while the herbs of power are on her.

Insanity

Exorcism and incantations by a witch-doctor is another remedy, but as it is a laborious undertaking, a good supply of whiskey is always provided for the adept. When any person in the village showed signs of madness, this man was sent for, and, after a good pull at the whiskey, the caster out of devils began his exorcism by pouring forth a torrent of gibberish in a loud voice, which he called Latin prayers; while at the same time he dashed holy water all over the room and the patient. Then, taking a stout blackthorn stick, he proceeded to thrash the demented person most vigorously, the patient being held firmly all the time by three or four of the friends or neighbors. When the poor victim was half stupefied, and unable even to yell any longer, the operator announced that the devil had gone out of him; but as the evil spirit was still lurking somewhere about, he must be expelled by force or magic. Whereupon he commenced to whirl the blackthorn stick round in all directions, striking everything, animate and inanimate, that lay in his way, as if crazed with fury; especially beating the doors, by which, he said, the devil might escape, and he was determined to have a good blow at him; and all the time, during the process of beating, he kept on reciting the gibberish Latin in a loud, strong voice, fortifying his efforts at exorcism by frequent appeals to the whiskey jar.

A singular case of attempted cure took place lately in Roscommon. A young man named Davy Flynn became suddenly raving mad, or 'elfstricken' as the people say, and the great witchman of the place was sent for one Sunday morning in all haste. He found him bound hand and foot, and foaming at the mouth, while five or six strong men were trying to hold him down; and a great crowd was gathered round the door, who declared that the wretched madman was not Davy Flynn at all, the handsome Davy, once the pride of the village for beauty and strength, but a fairy demon who had taken his shape. So the witch-man having examined him, and performed sundry strange rites and invocations, pronounced bis opinion that the lunatic was certainly not Davy Flynn, but an old French charger, a fine stalwart horse in his time, once belonging to a French general who came to Ireland long ago in the time of the troubles; and to keep the real man alive, who was now in Fairyland, the substitute must be well fed with the proper food for a horse.

On bearing this the friends ran for a sheaf of oats, and crammed the straw down the wretched maniac's throat, after which the exorcist prepared for his mortal combat with the devil, aided of course by the poteen, five kegs of which were brought in for the general strengthening of the company. The operator first tied a white apron over his shoulders, then, with a wave of the band in the form of a cross, he commanded silence. After which, be began the invocation by a volley of gibberish Latin, thundered forth between the occasional draughts of whiskey, while poor Davy had only a bucket of cold water thrown on his head, to which he responded by terrible cries.

At last the people got tired of the work, and one of them secretly cat the cord of the halter, which held the supposed French charger, while the witch-man was busy over the poteen. Davy, thus finding himself free, sprang at the doctor as if he would tear him to pieces, on which a panic seized the crowd, who rushed from the house, the witchman following, while the maniac leaped after them with hideous yells and curses. At length the maniac was secured and tied down by a strong rope till the magistrate arrived, who ordered him off to the Roscommon Lunatic Asylum, whither he was at once taken, and where he eventually died, to the great relief of his friends, who really believed that he was the old French charger, and that till the death of the demon-substitute, poor Davy had no chance of being released from the bondage he was under in Fairyland.

For Lumbago

Dog-fern roots and shamrocks should be cleaned and pounded well, then mixed with butter- made on May mornin- and holy salt, till a kind of paste is formed. This is rubbed all over the back, while the Lord's Prayer is said, and the Hail Mary; and the paste is by no means to be washed off, but left till the cure is perfected.

For the Liver Complaint

The leaves of plantain, wild sage, the shamrock and dock-leaf, with valerian and the flower of the daisy, are to be plucked by the person before sunrise, and fasting, on Mondays and Wednesdays, while Hail Mary is said, and the Paternoster; all these are to be boiled and strained, and the herbs afterwards to be carefully burned. A glassful of the liquor to be taken twice a day.

For Dysentery

Woodbine and maiden-hair, pounded and boiled in new milk, with oatmeal, and taken three times a day, the leaves to be afterwards burned.

ANCIENT CURES, CHARMS, AND USAGES OF IRELAND

ANCIENT CURES

(From an Irish Manuscript in the Royal Irish Academy, dated about 1450.)

For the Falling Sickness

Put salt and white snails into a vessel for three nights, add 7 lb. woodbine leaves, and mix them to a paste; a poultice of this applied for nine days will cure.

Or, the heart of a crow, beaten up with his blood, and drank for nine days, will relieve the disease.

Or, a plaster made of mandragora and ground ivy, boiled and laid upon the head. If the patient sleeps lie will do well, and if not, he will not.

Or, a band of the fresh skin of a wolf worn round the body as a girdle, and as long as the patient wears it he will be free from the falling sickness.

Or, pour wine upon a pound of hemlock, fresh gathered, and let it be drank while the person is in the fit.

Or, three hairs of a milk-white greyhound to be tied up and worn on the neck as an amulet. This keeps the fit away. The scribe who copied these receipts says of himself, "I am Conlan Mac Liagh son of: the doctor, and in the Monastery of Tuam I am this 14th day of the moon's age, and a thousand years, four hundred years, and nine years the age of the Lord." Pettigrew, in his interesting book on medical superstitions, mentions the ancient idea that black hellebore was to be plucked, not cut, and this with the right hand, which was then covered with the robe, while the herb was secretly conveyed to the left hand. The person gathering it, also, was to be clad in white, and to offer a sacrifice of bread and wine. He also mentions that vervain, one of the sacred herbs of the Irish, was to be gathered on the rising of the Dog-star, when neither sun nor moon was shining, an expiatory sacrifice of fruit and honey being previously offered to the earth. Hence the power of vervain to cure fevers, eradicate poison, and render the possessor invulnerable. And he makes mention of the virtues of the elder tree as being widely known for effecting a cure in cases of epilepsy; also the use of spiders and their webs for curing ague, applied in the same manner as is usual with the Irish. Barton, in his 'Anatomy of Melancholy,' mentions having himself used a plaster of spiders, the web being effective for the staunching of blood, as also the moss from a dead man's skull brought over from Ireland,

A porridge advised by Dianecht, chief physician of the Tuatha-de-Dauans, has been handed down through the centuries for relief of ailments of the body, as cold, phlegm, throat cats, and the presence of living things in the body, as worms. It consists of hazel-buds, dandelion, chickweed, and wood sorrel, all boiled together with oatmeal. This porridge to be taken morning and evening, when the cold and the trouble will soon disappear. Also a poultice of yellow baywort tied round the throat is excellent as a cure for the throat cats.

According to Dianecht, there are fourteen disorders of the stomach, and he gave recipes for all, consisting mostly of plants and herbs. Against witchcraft he ordered a potion to be made of the roots of the alder tree and the roots of the apple tree that grow downward in the earth. These to be boiled with the brains of a wild bog, and drank fasting, till the bewitched person casts up the evil thing: that was in the stomach.

ANCIENT CURES, CHARMS, AND USAGES OF IRELAND

To Cure a Fairy-stricken Child

Make a good fire, throw into it a handful or more of certain herbs ordered by the fairy-women; wait till a great smoke rises, then carry the child three times round the fire, reciting an incantation against evil, and sprinkling holy water all around. But during the process no door must be opened, or the fairies would come in to see what you were doing. Continue reciting the incantation till the child sneezes three times; then you may know that the fairy spell is broken, and the child has been redeemed from fairy thralldom for evermore. It is good, however, in addition, to tie a small bag round his neck, with three rounds of red ribbon or thread, containing a nail from the shoe of an ass and some hair of a black cat, and let this be worn for a year and a day.

A black cat without any white spot has great power either for or against witchcraft, and the hair must be taken from a cat of this description, for the demons fear it. Also, about midnight, give the child a drink mixed with the blood of a crowing hen; then he will be safe from fairy, or demon, or the evil of witchcraft.

For Deafness

Take the cowslip, roots, blossom, and leaves, clean them well, then bruise and press them in a linen cloth, add honey to the juice thus pressed out, put it in a bottle, and pour a few drops into the nostrils and ears of the patient, he lying on his back. Then, after some time, turn him on his face till the water pours out, carrying away whatever obstruction lay on the brain. This may be repeated for three days. Or fold up two eels in a cabbage-leaf, place them on the fire till they are soft then press out the juice and drop it into the ears.

ANCIENT CURES, CHARMS, AND USAGES OF IRELAND

But for ordinary disease there is nothing so good as the native poteen, for it is peculiarly adapted to the climate, and, as the people say, it keeps away ague and rheumatism, and the chill that strikes the heart; and if the gaugers would only let the private stills alone, not a bit of sickness would there be in the whole country round.

For Falling Sickness

No one should touch the person in the fit, only the man who works the charm. He first takes a bundle of unbleached linen yarn, and ties it round the patient, then cuts his hair, and the finger and toe nails; these clippings he gathers together and burns with the linen yarn. The ashes are then divided into two parts, after which the patient is laid flat on the earth and two holes are made, one at his head the other at his feet; into these are poured the divided ashes, while a harrow-pin is placed over all. So they leave him for a day and a night. And thus the falling sickness is buried for ever in that spot, never to rise up again while the ashes and the iron remain untouched.

Hydrophobia

Many of the cures, however, used by the people and the witch-doctors are not merely superstitious practices, but are based upon the accurate knowledge of herbs, and their mystic power on the human frame, which the Irish have possessed in all ages from the remotest times. For the rules and tenets of this primitive science have been transmitted orally through countless generations, with sacred reverence and solemn care, chiefly in the direct line of special families, who are the trusted guardians of the mysteries, and are bound by strict custom and traditional law not to divulge the secrets of herbal lore, except to the eldest son of the eldest son in direct succession.

ANCIENT CURES, CHARMS, AND USAGES OF IRELAND

In the County Cavan, the MacGowans, for instance, have a wonderful but secret cure for hydrophobia, known only to themselves, and acquired in this way: About one hundred and fifty years ago, two brothers of the name, living at opposite sides of the lake, used frequently to cross over in their boat to visit each other. One day a strange dog came swimming towards them and was lifted into the boat, but he instantly bit one of the brothers severely, and showed all the signs of decided madness. The young man gave himself up for lost, and wandered about the fields all night, till at last, overcome by fatigue, he lay down in his own garden and fell asleep. Then and there a dream came to him, that under his head grew a herb that would cure him, if prepared in a certain way revealed to him as in a vision.

On awakening, he at once sought for the herb, and having found it, to his great joy, set about the preparations for the potion exactly as it had been shown to him in the dream. The result was his perfect restoration from the fatal disease; and the strange story, having got abroad, the MacGowans became famous throughout the country for the cure of hydrophobia; large sums being paid to them for the exercise of their skill and knowledge. Thus they amassed a deal of money, for the wonderful herb seldom failed to cure the terrible malady; but no amount of money could tempt the brothers to reveal the name of the herb or the mode of preparation. This great secret remains, therefore, a mystery to this day, known only to the head of the MacGowans, who preserves the tradition, and will transmit it only to his eldest son.

But to ensure a perfect cure, certain rules and orders must be rigidly observed. First, the patient must be brought under care within nine days after the attack, before the hydrophobia has become virulent; secondly, he must not cross water during the progress of the cure. Quite recently a curious case happened which tested the power of the MacGowans, and excited the greatest interest throughout the country. A pet cat, belonging to a farmer's family, suddenly showed signs of savage ferocity, and flew at every one, inflicting severe bites. Sis of the children were laid up, and even the farmer himself was attacked before the animal could be killed, Evidently the beast was mad, and, in terror of the consequences, the family sent an urgent request to the MacGowans to come and help them. Three brothers of the name were living at the time, and the eldest agreed to go and try the cure, if fifty shillings were paid down to him before starting. This was a large sum for the farmer to give; but as six of the children were lying half dead from fright, he consented, and paid the money. MacGowan at once set forth on his mission of mystic healing, bringing with him two kegs of liquid, each containing about five gallons, also a large stock of garlic and hazel-nuts. The fluid was of a green color, and very nauseous to the taste. The people said it was made of the Atherlus (ground-ivy) which has singular mystic properties; but MacGowan kept strict silence on the subject, and no one dared to ask him a question as to the nature of the ingredients.

The family, meanwhile, were ordered to provide two stone of barley-meal and three pounds of butter, and with these cakes were to be made, moistened with the fluid from the keg, of which also the patients were to drink copiously; and during the three days appointed for the cure they were to have no other sustenance, save the barley cakes and the green fluid. If at the end of that time the cure was not effected, then the patients would surely die, their only chance was over, nothing more could be done to help them. Happily, however, the cure was quite successful. The children were all restored, and, consequently, the fame of the MacGowans increased, and no end of presents and money were sent to them in addition to the sum paid down. Still the head of the race resisted all entreaties to reveal the name of the herb or the secret of the green fluid, and to this day no man nor mortal, not even the priest himself, has ever obtained a knowledge of the mystery, save only the eldest son of the eldest son in each successive generation of the MacGowan family.

But other modes of curing the bite of a mad dog are used in different districts; one is to apply some of the hair of the dog to the wound and leave it there, bound tightly, till all danger is over. Another is to take out the liver of the dog, grind it to powder, then mix with water, and give it to the patient to drink.

In old times, in Ireland, people afflicted with canine madness were put to death by smothering between two feather beds; the near relatives standing round until asphyxia was produced, and death followed.

MALEFIC CHARMS

Not only are charms and incantations employed for curing disease, but they are also used to induce disease and death, in the form of maledictions and curses, and in the name of the Evil One. A sheaf of corn is sometimes buried with a certain form of dedication to Satan, in the belief that as the corn rots in the ground, so will the person wither away who is under the curse.

Another form of malediction is to bury a lighted candle by night in a churchyard, with certain weird ceremonies. A young village girl, who had been treated badly by her lover, determined on revenge, and adopted this mode of curse upon him. He was a fine, healthy young fellow; but suddenly he began to pine and dwindle away, and then every one knew that the girl must have buried a candle against him. Great efforts were made to induce her to tell where it was buried, but she resisted all entreaty. At last, however, the candle was found, and the man had to eat it in order to neutralize the curse. Yet even this disagreeable remedy was of no avail, for the young man still continued to pine away, and in a short time he lay dead.

Maledictions

Epidemic diseases that will carry off an entire family can also be produced by the devil's magic, and smiths and old women are generally adepts in the black art. St. Patrick prayed to be delivered from smiths, women, and Druids; and even to the present time the smith is considered powerful in the working of charms, either for a blessing or a curse, and the peasants are cautious not to offend him.

The Lusmore, or Fairy-finger, is a deadly poison, and sometimes has been used in malice to produce convulsions in children.

In the case of a sudden fainting or swoon, the individual is supposed to be struck by a curse, and if he is unable to answer questions, he is tried with a grannoge, or hedgehog, and if it erects the spine it is a sure sign that the person is under the influence of the devil. Or the suspected person is wrapped in a woman's red cloak, with the hood over the head, and laid in a grave cut two feet deep. There he remains some hours covered with clay, all but the face, and if he becomes delirious and raves, then the people know that the devils are round him, and his death is considered certain.

Imbas forosma (the knowledge that enlightens) was a weird and fearful pagan ceremony by which evil was invoked, and men gained knowledge of the future after offerings made to their idol gods. The performance was accompanied by strange and solemn incantations and mystic rites, but all of too terrible a nature to be revealed to the people. They were known only to the Druid priests, and by them held sacred.

If an infant is very small and weakly, it is supposed to be a fairy changeling, and under a curse. To test its nature, the child is placed upon a shovel before the fire. If it is a fairy imp, it will assuredly, after a little while, fly up the chimney, and disappear; but, while waiting for the solution of the question, the poor baby is often so dreadfully burned that it dies in great torture, though its cries are heard with callous indifference by the family around.

The Dead Hand

To obtain the power and secrets of witchcraft, it is necessary to visit a churchyard at midnight, and cut off the hand of a recently buried corpse with your own hand. This is preserved by drying or smoking, and can then be used with great and fatal effect. Old women are known as the strongest tools of the devil, and as having the most fatal powers of witchcraft. These witch-women are recognized at once by their glittering eyes and long, skeleton fingers; and if they have a dead hand in their possession, their influence is irresistible. If a witch-woman overlooks a beautiful child, it is doomed to die. If she overlooks the churn, the butter will be carried off to her own churn, though she has nothing but water in it. Beware of her.

When she enters the place, put a red coal under the churn, and tie a branch of the rowan tree on the child's cradle, and a red string on the cow's tail then they are safe. Every one who enters while churning is going on should take a turn with the dash, and say: "God bless the work" but a witch woman dare not say the words; therefore, if she refuses, she is known at once to be fatal and unlucky. Stroking by the hand of a dead man can cure many diseases. It has also the power to bring butter to the churn, if the milk is stirred round nine times with it while a witch-prayer is recited. Bat many awful things must be done, and evil rites practiced, before the witch-words can be learned and uttered.

WITCHCRAFT

An oath taken upon a skull brought from the churchyard is used for clearing from guilt. But should the oath be taken falsely, the sin will rest upon the race to the seventh generation, and all the sins of the man whose skull was used for the clearing will be upon the head of the false swearer also. There are two stones in Joyce country, Connemara, and if any one who is falsely maligned turns these stones while he prays a prayer against the wrong-doer, the prayer will be granted, and some evil luck will fall on the wrong-doer as a punishment from the hand of God.

If a young man is suddenly taken with weakness and depression of spirits, it is believed that a field mouse crept down his throat while he lay sleeping under the hayrick, and to cure him he must be well beaten, in the name of the Trinity, with a stick cut from a tree, in the hollow of which a field-mouse lay hidden. And, after the beating, the mouse is struck by the same stick till it dies.

The Evil Eye

If any one suspected of the evil eye looks fixedly at you, say at once: "The curse be upon thine eye." The evil-eye influence is particularly strong at Beltane (May Eve). And it is then advisable to sprinkle oatmeal on the cow's back, and to bleed the cattle and taste of the blood. In old times, the men and women were likewise bled, and their blood was sprinkled on the ground; but this practice has now died out, even in the western islands, though sacrifice through blood is always considered sacred and beneficial. The blight on cattle comes from some individual whose glance has a natural malignant power. You may know such persons at once by their lowering brows and sunken eyes. Distrust them, they are evil. Persons of defective baptism are also dangerous, for the devil already claims them for his own.

To break the spell of the evil eye, drive the cattle at once to a holy well, and make them drink of the blessed water. But if in going they chance to look at a graveyard, the cure will not succeed. Prayers, also, must be recited while the cattle are drinking at the well, and through the prayer of faith the spell will be broken.

Superstitions

The popular superstitions of the Irish people seem to have remained unchanged from the earliest time to the present day. A writer who traveled in Ireland in 1690- Lawrence Eochard, of Christ College, Cambridge- mentions several of the usages which none of the peasants would dare to transgress, that came under his observation.

"The people," he says, "think it wrong to rub down or curry their horses, or to gather grass to feed them, upon Saturdays. They also esteem her wicked and a witch who asks for fire on May morning, and butter would only be given to a sick body, and then with a curse. If butter is stolen, they cut away some of the thatch from over the door and cast it into the fire, believing that so the butter will be restored. When going out in the morning, they are very careful who they meet first, for good luck, or ill luck, may come for the day in that manner to a man. Before sowing the corn, some salt is flung on the earth; and in the towns, when a magistrate first enters on his office, the wives and daughters, along the street, fling wheat and salt down on him and his followers."

ANCIENT CURES, CHARMS, AND USAGES OF IRELAND

Food of the Irish

He also notes the very simple diet of the people, and their temperance as to food. "The Irish," he says, "feed much upon herbs, watercresses, shamrocks, mushrooms, and roots. They also take beef broth, and flesh, sometimes raw, from which they have pressed out the blood. They do not care much for bread, but they give the corn to their horses, of whom they are very careful. They also bleed their kine, and as the blood stiffens to a jelly, they stew it with butter, and eat it with great relish, washing it down with huge draughts of usquebaugh."

Among the stimulants recommended by the later Irish physicians, we find saffron named as 'the most excellent of tonics' also aqua vitae and sugar, with bread soaked in it, that it may not harm the brain, is specially advised as an energetic strengthener of the organs of the body.

For the Memory

White frankincense beaten up with white wine is profitable for the brain and the stomach, and an excellent cordial may be made of one part gentian, and two parts centaury, bruised well together, and mixed with distilled water for a drink. But these things are for the learned and the aristocrats. The peasants still cling to their simple herbal cures and mystic charms, and the ancient usages of the old world times.

To ascertain the result of a fever the people will take a black cock, split him open, and apply the halves, while still hot, to the soles of the feet. Should they stick on, the patient will recover; but if the pieces fall to the ground, then death is certain. If any feathers of wild fowl be in a bed the patient will not sleep, and his death will be disturbed and painful. The only help is to hang a horse-shoe on the bed, or to place the sick person's shoe face downward.

SUPERSTITIONS

On St. Bridget's day a crop of peeled rushes is nailed to the door, and a mat of fresh hay is laid down for the Saint to kneel on, in case she comes to pray for any sick member of the family. St. Bridget was very high tempered and haughty in her ways. One day she came to attend mass at St. Mark's chapel, but found, when she arrived, that the ceremony was all over. Then she was angry, being accustomed to much reverence, and asked the Saint, indignantly, why he had not waited for her arrival, to which St. Mark answered: "For no man nor woman shall I delay the holy rites of the Church." Then Bridget grew more angry, and prayed that a lake might cover the Saint's court and chapel. And so it was, for the waters began to rise till the court, and chapel, and the Saint's cell were all submerged, and the great lake was formed as it now exists. But once every seven years, on St. Mark's day, the bells can be heard ringing in the lake, and the chant of the choristers; and of a summer's day, down deep in the water, can be plainly seen a heap of stones, and the people know that they are looking on the ruins of St. Mark's chapel, banned and doomed by the power of the holy Bridget.

The Leprechaun

The little gray Leprechaun has the secret of hidden gold, and by the power of a certain herb he can discover it and thus become master of unlimited wealth. But no one has ever yet obtained from the tricksy little sprite the name of the herb or the words of the charm which reveal the hidden treasure, only the Leprechaun has the knowledge. There are also herbs of grace to be gathered on May morning which give wealth to him who knows the proper form of incantation; but if he reveals the mystery he dies. So the adepts keep the secret, being afraid of the doom. Yet the peasantry still make constant efforts to find the hidden gold, and many curious rites are practiced by them to obtain a knowledge of the mystic herbs.

Concerning Trees

The most sacred trees in Ireland are the yew tree, the rowan, the hazel, and the willow. The hazel is the most effective against demon power and witchcraft. It was by the use of a hazel wand that St. Patrick drove out the serpents from Ireland, one only escaping, who plunged into the Great Lake at Killarney, and remains there to this day crying to be released. And with a hazel stick a person can draw a circle round himself, within which no evil thing can enter- fairy, or demon, or serpent, or evil spirit. But the stick must be cut on May morning, and before sunrise, to make it powerful.

The rowan tree is very sacred, and branches of it should be hung on May morning over the child's cradle, and over the churn and the door, to keep away evil spirits and evil hands. The blessed power of the hazel and the rowan is firmly believed in to the present day, and is still used as the best safeguard against witches; for the Irish, like their Persian ancestors, are fervent tree-worshipers, and no tree is considered malignant in its influence. The willow is thought to have a soul in it which speaks in music; for this reason the Irish harps were generally made of the wood. Brian Borohm's ancient harp, still in existence, is made of the willow tree.

Whoever has the four-leaved shamrock has good luck in all things. He cannot be cheated in a bargain, nor deceived, and whatever he undertakes will prosper. It enlightens the brain, and makes one see and know the truth; and by its aid wondrous things can be done. So the people say, "Whoever has the four-leaved shamrock can work miracles." But it must never be shown to man nor mortal, or the power would exist no more.

The Sacred Tree

It is very dangerous and unlucky to cut down an ancient tree made sacred by the memory of a saint. One cold, winter's day, during the hungry times, a farmer was tempted to cut down a few branches of a huge alder that shadowed the ancient well of St. Moling; when, on looking back, he saw his house in flames. Immediately he rushed to the spot, but, on reaching home, found that all was safe and no flames were visible. So he returned to his work of cutting off the branches, when again the red flames rose high over his cottage, and again he hastened to the spot to extinguish the fire; but with the same result- all was safe at his home.

So, determined not to be disappointed a third time in getting the branches, he returned to the tree, and lopped off as much as he required from the sacred alder, and carried the bundle safe home; when, to his dismay, he found that the cottage was burned to the ground, and he was left without a roof over his head.

The Briar

Great virtue is attributed to the briar, especially in cases of a sprain, or dislocation; the species bearing a reddish flower being the best for use. A strong twig of this is taken, about a yard long and split evenly from end. to end. The pieces are then held by two men with clean hands, about three feet apart- the mystery-man pronouncing an incantation, and waving his hands over them until the twigs seem endowed with life, and rise up and approach each other till they touch; then a piece is cut off at the point of contact, and bound firmly over the sprain, the mystery-man all the time never ceasing his incantations, nor the waving of his hands. The ligature is left on for three days, after which time the sprain is found to be perfectly cured; but the power of the split sticks is entirely neutralized, should either of the men holding them be illegitimate.

The buds of the briar are used in spring to make a refreshing drink for the sick, and the roots in winter. The roots are boiled for twelve hours in an earthen vessel, then a small cupful of the liquid is administered frequently to the patient, who, after some time, falls into a deep sleep from which he will awake perfectly cured.

Concerning Birds

Everything in nature, above and around them, exercises a mysterious influence over the Irish mind, and is connected, the people believe, with their fortune and destiny, either for good or evil. Trees are venerated and held to be sacred and beneficial; but, strange to say, birds are not trusted, as if some malign spirit were in them. They come and go, according to the popular belief, with significant messages from the unseen world of good or bad omen, but generally with warning and prophecies of doom. The water-wagtail is particularly disliked, for it has strange mystical powers, and its presence always forebodes something fatal.

A gentleman in the County Cork happened to be suffering from an attack of fever; but no danger was apprehended until one morning early, when a water-wagtail came to the window and tapped furiously at the glass with his bill, as if trying to break the glass and enter the room. For three mornings this was repeated, by which time the sick man's nerves were so completely shaken that he gave himself up for lost, and in four days he was dead. But, to the surprise and terror of the family, the bird still continued to come each morning and strike the window as before. Then, the wife, who was kneeling by her husband's coffin in prayer, rose up and said: "Behold! the spirit of doom has come for another of the family; one death is not enough; let us watch and pray." And the evil came as foretold, for when returning from his father's funeral, the eldest son was thrown violently from the carriage, the horses having taken fright in some unaccountable manner, and the young man was carried home dead to his unhappy mother.

The robin redbreast is the only bird looked upon with favor and veneration by the peasantry; for they believe that he once hid the Lord Jesus from his enemies, by covering Him with moss, but the water-wagtail plucked away the moss and so discovered our Lord to the Jews; for which act the bird has even been considered unholy and unlucky, while the robin is held sacred, and no one would dare to injure it.

When a raven is seen hovering round a cottage, evil is near, and a death may follow, or some great disaster, therefore to turn away ill luck, say at once: "May fire and water be in you, bird of evil, and may the curse of God be on your head for ever and ever."

If anyone is sick in the house, and the cock crows with his head to the fire, recovery may be expected; but if he crows with his head to the door, then death is certain. If a hen crows on the roost it is a sign that the fairies have struck it, and the head of the hen must be immediately cut off and flung on the ground, or one of the family will surely die before the year is out.

Never disturb the swallows, wherever they may build, and neither remove nor destroy their nests; for they are wise birds, and will mark your conduct either for punishment or favor.

The first time you hear the cuckoo, look down at your

feet; if a hair is lying there you will live to comb your own gray locks at a good old age. There is an old rhyme respecting this bird:

> "If a cuckoo sits on a bare thorn,
> You may sell your cow and buy corn;
> But if she sits on a green bough,
> You may sell your corn and buy a cow."

Superstitions

When a person is dying, twelve rush-lights are lighted and stuck in a bowl of meal, and left burning till the death takes place; then the candles are extinguished, and the meal is given to the first pauper who passes the door. The corners of the sheet, also, that wrapped the corpse, are carefully cut off and laid by as charms for disease. The pins, likewise, used in laying out the dead, are preserved reverentially, for they have great power as mystic charms ever after. Among fatal signs, the most fatal is to break a looking-glass, for then it is certain that someone in the house will die before the year is out. And there is no mode of averting the evil fate. This superstition still holds its power over the people; indeed, among all classes to the present day the omen is looked upon with dread, and a firm belief in its fatal significance.

To break the spell of witchcraft, it is good to eat of barley cakes over which the exorcist has said an incantation. But the patient must eat of them only on Mondays and Thursdays, and the Monday following; never on a Friday.

On Twelfth night the people make a cake of yellow clay taken from a churchyard, then stick twelve bits of candle in it, and recite their prayers,, kneeling round, until all the lights have burned down. A name is given to each light, and the first that goes out betokens death to the person whose name it bears, before the year is out.

On Candlemas night the same trick is practiced; twelve lighted candles are named after the family, the first whose light burns out, dies first; and so on to the last, who will be the survivor of all. On Ash Wednesday, every one is marked on the forehead with the blessed ashes, and the black mark is retained carefully through the day, the priest himself having touched the brow with his finger. Also, a coal is brought from the priest's house to kindle the fire, for the consecrated coal brings good fortune to the house and the inmates.

It is good to cut the hair at the new moon, and by the light of the moon itself; but never should the hair be cut on a Friday, for it is the most unlucky day of all the year, and no one should begin a journey, or move into a new house, or commence business, or cut out a new dress on a Friday; and, above all, never bring a cat from, one house to another on a Friday. The creation of Adam, the Fall, the expulsion from Eden, and the death of Christ, all took place on a Friday; hence its evil repute and fatal influence, above all other days of the week, upon human actions. But the fairies have great power on that day, and mortals should stay at home after sunset, for the fairies always hold their revels upon Fridays, and resent being interfered with or troubled by the human presence.

It is unlucky to meet a red-haired man or woman the first thing in the morning; but a freckled, red haired woman is particularly dangerous. Should she be in your path on first going out, turn back at once, for danger is in the way. Some say that Judas Iscariot had red hair, hence the tradition of its evil augury. It is unlucky to offer your left hand in salutation, for there is an old saying: "A curse with the left hand to those we hate, but the right hand to those we honor."

ANCIENT CURES, CHARMS, AND USAGES OF IRELAND

It is unlucky to sit down thirteen to dinner, for one of the party will certainly die before the year is out. This is a most wide-spread superstition, and extends to all classes from the highest to the lowest. It probably originated from the fact that Judas was the thirteenth at the Last Supper, and the evil was in his heart as he sat at meat. There are some days in the week considered unpropitious by the people for certain work or projects. Thus, no one should undertake any business of importance on Wednesdays or Fridays, nor set out on a journey, nor get married; and should the ancient superstition he disregarded, evil will fall on the sinner, and whether it comes from heaven or hell, come it will, so the peasants believe, for the fairies are out on those nights, and have their revels and dances, and no mortal should trouble them. But the fairies never have three parties in the week, for that is the number of the Trinity, and is sacred and holy; so they leave the other days free to men. There is a popular rhyme concerning days and children:

> "Monday's child fair in the face,
> Tuesday's child fair of grace,
> Wednesday's child lone and sad,
> Thursday's child merry and glad,
> Friday's child must work for a living,
> Saturday's child is Godly given, but
> Sunday's child will go straight to heaven."

Burying Grounds

In old times it was thought right and proper to have separate burying-grounds for the different classes. There was one for aged strangers, another for infants who died unbaptized, for they could not be admitted into consecrated ground. Suicides were buried separately, in a place called, 'The Wounded Man's Grave.' Women who died in child-birth had also a special burial-ground, and the men were buried alone. In the County Tyrone there is a male burying-ground, and if a woman enters it and stands upon a grave, she will assuredly die before the year is out. Consequently, no living woman will pass the gate, only the dead men. The dead are very strict as to form and usage, and would all rise up from their graves if one, not of their class, were laid among them.

Also, if anything lies heavy on the conscience of a dead man, he will appear to his people and give them no rest till the disturbing cause is removed. A very respectable aged man having died near Dunmore Castle some few years ago, his brother buried him with all honor in the graveyard near by; but the corpse would not rest quiet. At night, and in lonely places, the ghost would appear and fix his dead eyes on the brother, but say no word, and look so mournful, that the poor man had no joy in life and knew not what to do. Then he consulted the priest at last, and his reverence gave him some holy water blessed and consecrated by himself with special prayers, and told him to take the flask with him at night to the place where he usually met the ghost, and question him as to the cause of his disquiet. So the man went as desired, and drew a circle round himself as he stood, and poured the holy water all over the place. And at twelve o'clock exactly the ghost appeared; and when he got within the circle the man felt brave enough to speak, for he knew he was protected by the holy water. So he asked the ghost: "Why have you left the grave to trouble me?" Then the ghost told him that only one thing prevented him getting to heaven, and he would never have rest unless this sin were removed from him, for the thread that sewed his grave-clothes was stolen thread, and the angels wouldn't touch him while it was there, so he had to wander about, and had no place of rest either on earth or in heaven, and he bade the brother go to the grave and rip the clothes, and take away all the thread and burn it, and get a mass said for the repose of his soul, after which he would have rest. And all this the brother did, even as he was desired, and the ghost was seen no more.

A corpse must not be touched by any hand, nor keened over, until two hours at least have passed after death, for the soul must be given time to settle quietly in its new place of rest; and the voice of the mourners might quicken the dead into a brief return to temporal life, when the pangs of a second death would be greater even than those of the first. The body is then washed with soap and water, and dried with a linen cloth; and the use being over, the water is spilled, and the cloth buried in a hidden place in the earth, where no foot will tread and no eye will behold them till a twelvemonth has passed by; for if any person stood upon the ground where the water was spilled; he would be fated to wander about the fields all' night, not knowing where to find his house till the cock-crow in the early morn.

Superstitions

When the body is laid in the coffin, the priest sanctifies a handful of earth and sprinkles it over the corpse. And this is done because, if any self-murdered person were brought to the churchyard to be buried, all the dead would turn in their coffins, unless only those on whose bodies the blessed earth had been sprinkled by the priest. If the face of a first-born child is turned downwards in the coffin, the parents will never have any more children.

Never cut an infant's nails till it is a twelvemonth old, or it will be light-fingered, and addicted to stealing.

Never get married in harvest, or you will have no rest from worries and troubles, and will always be overworked, and laden with cares and anxieties all your life long.

A new-married couple should retire to rest at the same

time, for if the bride were left alone, the fairies would come and steal her away for the sake of her fine clothes.

When a person sneezes, the people around say at once: "The blessing of God and the Holy Mary be on you," otherwise the fairies would do some evil turn. Or they say: "The consecration be upon you," meaning the holy water. This will at once avert all fairy spite and malice. It is very unlucky to meet a weasel coming towards you in the early morning, and you should at once spit at him, for if he spits at you first, a great danger will fall on you before the sun sets. Yet, you must never kill a weasel; it is fatal, and will bring sure destruction on yourself, for the whole family of the murdered weasel will take vengeance and cause something dreadful to happen to you within the year.

When changing your residence, it is unlucky to bring a cat with you, especially across a stream, and a red and white cat is particularly ominous and dangerous. If a black cat comes of her own accord to your house, keep her, she is a good spirit; but do not bring her, she must come freely, of her own good will. The tail of a black cat rubbed on the eyes has marvelous curative properties, and the blood of a black cat is largely used in all mystic cures for disease.

If a cow suddenly falls sick, without any apparent cause, it is believed that she has swallowed an insect of the beetle kind, called Derib, which lives in ditches and stagnant pools. The remedy is to strike the animal three times across the loins, with a garment belonging to any one of the name of Cassidy. But if a cow is bewitched by the fairies and gives no milk, the owner must lead her three times round one of the ancient stone monuments near a holy well, casting an elf stone each time on the heap. And if this is not successful, then elf stones must be tied up in a cloth with a piece of money, and thrown into a vessel of water for the animal to drink. Some butter, also, may be added to propitiate the saint of the well, and after this the cow will surely recover.

There is a large stone at Dunsang, County Louth, bearing a rude resemblance to a chair. This is called 'The Madman's Stone' and the people believe that if a lunatic is placed on it, seated, he will recover his reason.

At Portrane, County Dublin, is a well called 'The Chink Well,' which at high tide is covered by the salt water, yet always remains itself fresh and pure. Any one seeking a cure should leave a piece of bread on the brink of the well, and if this is carried away by the next tide the disease will depart also along with it. At the village of Dunas, County Clare, once the property of Sir Hugh Massy, is a well noted for many healing virtues, from having been blessed by St. Lenanus, who dwelt near it, and has left the impression of his hands and knees as he prayed on the flat rock near the brink. The people try to kneel in these indentations as they stoop to drink, and never fail to find relief if they touch the impression left by the Saint.

A most efficacious cure for disease of any kind is to eat a piece of the bread of which the Apostles gathered twelve baskets full after Christ's miracle of feeding the multitude. The wandering friars carry about with them some of this miraculous bread, and sell it to the people in small quantities for urgent cases, especially among the crowd surrounding the holy wells; for if the blessed bread is added to the power of the holy well, the cure cannot fail of success. The peasants have also great faith in the scapular, which is worn tied round the neck as a talisman or charm against all evil demons, fairies, or witches. If a woman is in great danger of death during her confinement, and is not wearing the scapular, she must be invested at once, and the midwife always carries one with her ready for the purpose. A strip of the skin of an ass and a piece of the hoof are also tied round her neck, in memory of the travail of the Holy Mother in the manger at Bethlehem. But if the woman is dying, the scapular must be at once removed, for if she dies with it on, she carries away the blessing out of it, and it has no more virtue until reblessed by the priest. It is generally taken from the dying woman by the nearest female relative, who reverently places it around her own neck, there to remain until she also has to give up her soul to God.

Until a woman has gone through the ceremony of churching, after the birth of her child, she is the most dangerous being on earth. No one should eat food from her hand, and myriads of demons are always around her trying to do harm, until the priest comes and sprinkles holy water over her. Even if she goes to the river to wash, the fish will all go away from her in tremor and fear. For fishes are a very pious race, and cannot bear to be touched by unholy hands ever since the mark of Christ's fingers was on them. Indeed, they were once by accident auditors of an argument against transubstantiation held by a heretic, and were so shocked at his language that they all left the river, and the disappointed angler could not help regretting that the fish were so very particular as to the tenets of the Holy Church.

If a man leave home after his wife's confinement, some of his clothes should be spread over the mother and infant, or the fairies will carry them both off. For the fairy queen desires, above all things, a mortal woman as a nurse for her fairy offspring. And if her own child happens to be an ugly little sprite, she will gladly change it for the beautiful human babe, who henceforth will live entirely in Fairyland, and never more see his kindred or home.

When a woman is nervous or hysterical, she is often supposed to be fairy-struck; but if the symptoms are severe, she is pronounced to be in Fairyland, while a simulacrum, or fairy sprite, has taken her place in the house, and assumed her features and appearance. Then the priest is sent for; but if his prayers are of no avail, the family apply to the fairy-doctor, who begins his operations by filling a vessel with oatmeal, over which he mutters an incantation. If half the oatmeal disappears suddenly, then he pronounces that a fairy is present in the woman's form, and the remainder of the meal being made into a cake, is given to her to eat; solemn incantations being recited all the time, while the doctor lays his hands on the head of the patient. This process is repeated for three days, after which the true woman comes back from Fairyland, and is able to resume her household duties, being perfectly restored in health. If a male child is born in Trinity week, he is fated to take away life, his own or another's. To break the fatality, a little bird is caught and held close in the child's hand till it dies. Then the danger is over, and the evil spell is broken through the sacrifice of the bird as an offering to death.

Omens

To break a mirror is the most unlucky accident that can happen. It portends many coming crosses and trials, and sometimes foretells a death. It happened once that a gentleman, who was just married, drove up in his carriage to the door of his residence with his bride ; his little niece, hearing the arrival, ran to the window and dashed back the glass door, never heeding that it struck a handsome pier-glass by the violent swing, till the broken pieces fell to the ground. Her nurse was terribly alarmed at first, but then hastily picking up two pieces of glass, she ran out to hide them in the folds of the bride's dress, before she entered the house, and this she accomplished while no one was minding her, in the hurry of the arrival. Thus the child was saved, for the ill luck was transferred to the bride, who had, indeed, a sad life after, of cares and crosses; but the little girl grew up well and happy, and was noted for her good fortune in all things she set her mind on.

The cricket is looked upon as a most lucky inmate of a house, and woe to the person who may happen to kill one; for all the other crickets will meet in general assembly and eat up the offender's clothes, as a just retribution for the loss of a friend and relation.

Every woman in charge of a dairy should wear three rings blessed in the name of the Trinity, one to guard from the wiles of women, the second from the wiles of men, the third from the wiles of witches.

The Nature of Fairies

In Connaught the people have many strange superstitions of great antiquity. If a child spills its tin of milk on the ground, the mother says: "That to the fairies, leave it to them and welcome," and the child is never scolded, lest that might bring ill luck. For the fairies hate everything that looks mean and niggardly, being themselves of a bright, free, joyous nature; except, indeed, the Banshee, who is the spirit of sorrow and doom. And the fairies like people who are kind and considerate, and who leave food on the dresser and fire in the grate at night for them when they hold their councils; yet not too much fire, for they dislike smoke, and the good woman of the house must never throw out water after dark, without saying; "Take care of the water" for the fairies are very nice in their ways, and resent any such awkward chance as might spoil their pretty gay caps and feathers. They also greatly desire human aid, and are very clever and acute in obtaining it. Sometimes they carry off a man at night, put him on a horse, jump up behind him, and away they go fleet as the wind. But when the man comes back in the morning to his home, wearied and exhausted, he finds that, instead of a splendid horse, he has only been riding a log of wood, or perhaps a sucking-calf, and he can hear the laughter of the fairies as he flings himself down on the hay to rest after their malicious tricks. Yet the fairies often strive to have human help in their battles, and, above all, a human leader; for whichever side has a living man for its general will surely gain the day; and they try to obtain him by sundry tricks, as in this way: They dress up an old broomstick like a man and place it in deep water, then, when any one goes over to examine it, they toss the broom into the stream and carry off the man.

But, after the battle, if he gains it for them, they send him back laden with fairy gifts, and he has good luck ever after. Though if he is unsuccessful, they strike him, and send him home lame of a leg or with a crooked neck. The fairies may be propitiated, but are never worshiped by the people, who look on them as inferior beings to themselves; and they know well that all the fairy spite against them is caused by envy and jealousy because man has been created immortal, while the Sidhe race is doomed to extinction at the last day. Bat saints and angels receive full homage from the people, and they are invoked against all evil influences with the most earnest faith and trust. The people are very suspicious of fairy influence being used for gain, and if a farmer among them makes more money than his neighbors, they become indignant and often do an injury to his cattle as a punishment. There was a man living in Innistush, one of the western islands, who had a wonderful cow with only one horn; but she gave more milk than any other cow on the island, and always came of herself to be milked. So the people said: "Surely he hath sold himself to the evil one for luck, but no luck will come to him though he gathers ever so much gold" and they determined to do him an ill turn. Now the man was out fishing one day, when a vision came to him that his cow was dead, and as he lamented he heard a voice saying; "Go to the great cave on the hill and call her three times, and she will answer you and come back to you."

So the man hastened home, and as he neared the house he heard a great cry, and there, sure enough, was his wife weeping and lamenting because the cow was dead; and all the women were round her, trying to comfort her.

"Whisht, Alanna," he said, "the cow is all safe. She is under a fairy spell and is hidden away in the great cave under the hill; but, never fear, for I'll put a stronger spell on her by the power I learned in my dream." So that same night he took fire with him and went to the cave, and called three times on the cow: "Come forth, come forth, come forth," but she came not. Then he lit the turf all round the cave and called out again: "See, I have the power of the fire and I will burn down the hill unless the cow is restored to me." Then a little man came forth and his face flamed with wrath. "May your fire be accursed," he said; "take your cow away with you, but never more will she do you any good, for the curse of the fairies is upon her."

And he entered the cave and led her forth. But she trembled, and began to moan when her master tried to lead her away. Then the farmer was sorely grieved, for he saw that she was bewitched, and would never leave the fairies and come with him. And as he turned away lamenting, and very sorrowful, a young girl came up close and whispered in his ear: "Ask for the spansel, or you will never get her back." On this the farmer called out again: "Bring me the spansel, or I'll burn down the hill and not leave a soul that is not scorched by the fire." So the old man came forth again from the cave looking still more wrathful, and he cried out fiercely: "Accursed be your fire for evermore. The spansel shall be yours. Only leave me in peace."

And he bade a young lad, who was by, to enter the cave and bring forth the spansel. So when the farmer got it, he was content; for the evil spell was broken at last through the judgment of fire. And the cow came back with her master, and gave milk enough ever after to keep him and his wife in plenty and comfort; and the neighbors were afraid to play any more wicked tricks, for they saw that a good man can conquer even the power of the fairies, and all the envy and malice of men, through wisdom and the help of God.

The exorcism by fire and water, these being the two most powerful elements in nature, is of great antiquity and is still held in high respect by the fairy-doctors. It was practiced by the Druids in their solemn rites, and St. Patrick in his conflict with the pagan priesthood made use of the double ordeal of fire and water.

As already stated, there is a prevalent belief that Friday is the most unlucky day of all the year, for the fairies are very powerful then, and mortal people should be very cautious about opening the door after sunset and allowing a stranger to enter the house. But there was a farmer's wife in Shark Island, who was so good and kindly, that she never refused a handful of meal or a light of the pipe to any wayfarer that passed her door. And one day (it chanced to be Friday) as she was churning, towards evening, a lame woman, with a red cloak wrapped about her head, tapped gently, and begged the good mistress would just let her come in and eat a bit, for she was very weary, and had traveled far.

"Come in and welcome" said Mrs. Sullivan, "and there is a seat ready for you by the fire," and she went on churning as the woman came in. Now there chanced to be a can of water just near the fire, and the old woman turned it over by accident as she sat down, and all the water ran under the churn. This, of course, was a sign of ill luck; but the woman expressed so much sorrow, that poor Mrs. Sullivan could not scold her nor turn her away, and she even gave her a drink of milk to comfort her.

"Now, Alanna," said the lame woman, "I'll not trouble you any more; but just put a little milk in my can to help me on the road when the thirst is on me, and give me a light of my pipe, and then I'll be off, for the sun is down, and I must meet my people on the hill before it grows dark."

"That I'll do and welcome," said the mistress of the house, "so here is the fill of your can for you of milk, and a good lump of butter, too, at the top, and now light your pipe and go in peace."

Then the lame woman rose up and took the can of milk with thanks. "And now, by your leave, before I go, I'll just light my pipe," she said, and with that she took a piece of burning sod from the fire, and carried it outside to light her pipe, and then went her way, throwing the fire on the road.

Some time after, the farmer came home, and his wife told him all that had happened. "Woman," he said, "you have destroyed our luck. You allowed a lame woman to come in here and sit down, while you were churning; you let the water be spilled on the floor under the churn; you gave away milk and butter on a Friday, and also allowed fire to be taken out of the house on a Friday by that lame witch; our luck is gone for ever by your folly." And so it was, for from that day the butter grew less and less, and there was so little money left in the house that the children cried from hunger, and there was nothing to give them to eat, and the poor mother was at her wits' end for sorrow, and worked like a slave for the morsel they had. But one evening, coming home late, she met the lame woman in the field, carrying her big can as before. "What have you got, now, in the can?" asked Mrs. Sullivan.

"Why, what else should it be but your own butter," said the lame woman; "see, the can is full to the top with the loveliest butter eyes could see, and all your own."

"But how can that be, good woman, for we have none—our luck is gone?" cried poor Mrs. Sullivan, weeping. "Well, I'll tell you, just in this way. Every morning, long before sunrise, while you are fast asleep, I milk the cow and carry off the milk in my big can here; and so I have always the richest butter in the whole island for myself and my people," and the lame woman laughed as she told her story.

"Oh, Maia, mother!" cried poor Mrs. Sullivan, in tears, "what am I to do, and my children dying of hunger, and not a bit of food in the house, and no money nor nothing?"

"Well now," said the lame woman, "don't fret, I shall have pity on you; for you were good to me the day I rested at your house. But take my advice, for I am wise, and what I say is true and must be done; go home and tie a red string on the cow's tail and another on her horns, and do not let her out before sunrise; this will keep her from the witches, my particular friends, and I'll bring them to another place for their milk and butter, so yours shall be safe. But mind, never again give away butter on a Friday; nor let water be spilled under the churn; nor let fire be taken out of your house on a Friday, for on that day the witches are powerful, and through the fire and water the spell of evil was made and laid upon you. Attend, therefore, to my words, for I am the head of the witches, and my word is law," and with that she disappeared and was seen no more. Then Mrs. Sullivan hastened home, wondering at the words, but she did as was desired and tied the red strips on the cow's tail and horns; and next day, to her great delight, she had her pail full of milk; and the churning went on even better than ever, and the butter was the richest and best in the whole country; for she always put a live coal under the churn before beginning, and on Fridays she watched the door carefully, and allowed no stranger to come in to carry away milk or fire, especially no lame woman and so the old luck came back, and the children laughed again and were happy, for they had enough of the best to eat; and the farmer forgave his wife; and, henceforth, they had plenty of money, and peace, and rest, and happiness.

The Banshee

The Ban-Sidhe, the fairy spirit of doom, never appears but to aristocrats. She is an appanage only of the highest families, who are always followed by the shadow of this spirit of death, supposed to be a beautiful young girl of the race, who cannot enter heaven until some other member of the family, who must be likewise young and beautiful, takes her place through death. Ban, or Van, means woman; and Vanitha, the lady of the house, in Sanskrit, as in Irish, comes from the root Van- to love, to desire. To this day the lady of the house is called The Vanitha by the Irish, the word having the same meaning as Venus, 'the loved one,' in its original signification.

At Lord O'Neil's residence, Shane's Castle, there is a room appropriated to the use of the Banshee, and she often appears there; sometimes shrouded and muffled in a dark, mist-like cloak. At other times, she is seen as a beautiful young girl, with long, red-gold hair, and wearing a green kirtle and scarlet mantle, brooched with gold, after the Irish fashion. There is no harm or fear of evil in her mere presence, unless she is seen in the act of crying; but this is a fatal sign, and the mournful wail is a sure and certain prophecy that the angel of death is waiting for one of the family.

The Demon Bride

The ancient churchyard of Truagh, County Monaghan, is said to be haunted by an evil spirit, whose appearance generally forebodes death. The legend runs that at funerals the spirit watches for the person who remains last in the graveyard. If it be a young man who is there alone, the spirit takes the form of a beautiful young girl, inspires him with an ardent passion, and exacts a promise that he will meet her that day month in the churchyard. The promise is then sealed by a kiss, which sends a fatal fire through his veins, so that he is unable to resist her caresses, and makes the promise required. Then she disappears, and the young man proceeds homewards; but no sooner has he passed the boundary wall of the churchyard, than the whole story of the evil spirit rushes on his mind, and he knows that he has sold himself, soul and body, for a demon's kiss. Then terror and dismay take hold of him, till despair becomes insanity, and on the very day month fixed for the meeting with the demon bride, the victim dies the death of a raving lunatic, and is laid in the fatal graveyard of Truagh.

In a recent case, where a young man was reported to have fallen under the influence of this weird temptation, the priest was sent for by the family to try if by his power he could absolve the victim from the promise given. Still no exorcism had any effect. On the very day of the intended meeting, the young man fell to the earth with the glare of madness in his eyes, and when they tried to lift him he was dead. But the evil spirit does not limit its operations to the graveyard; for sometimes the beautiful demon form appears at weddings or festivities, and never fails to secure its victims, by dancing them into the fever that maddens the brain, and too surely ends in death.

ST PATRICK'S DAY 17TH MARCH

St. Patrick, the great apostle, teacher, and guide of the Irish people out of the darkness of paganism, holds a most remarkable and eminent place in the early history of humanity. He was a man of culture and learning, and of extraordinary wisdom, power, and mental force. This is proved by his rapid and decisive overthrow of paganism and of the strong Druidic priesthood in Ireland, through the daring and successful measures he adopted for the establishment of Christianity.

Baal and Moloch fell before him at once, and he raised the Christian altar by the side of the pillar to the Sun God- an altar and a faith that have now remained fixed and fast for fourteen hundred years. Therefore on his day, the 17th of March, twenty millions of Irish all over the world celebrate the Saint's name, and honor his memory. When Patrick arrived in Ireland with his little band of faithful followers, it is told of him that he saw a dense ring of demons round the island, extending a six days' journey from it on every side. These obstructionists, however, he subdued without much difficulty; but, of all the doctrines he preached to the men of Erin the Irish found that forgiveness of injuries was the hardest, and the nation in this respect seems unchanged to this day. St. Bridget, afterwards the great Abbess of Kildare, was his first convert, and worked with him all through his apostolate; hence these two names were consecrated to the use of all the children born since in Ireland, and have become the expression of Irish nationality.

The opening of Patrick's mission was bold and grand. By the King's command no fire was to be lit in Erin on the morning of the Baal festival, until the Royal fire was first kindled at Tara, under pain of death; but Patrick, disdaining obedience, boldly lighted his Paschal fire on the hill of Slane, so that it could be seen by the whole country round. On this the King was wroth, and sent forth from Tara nine chariots and armed men to seize Patrick and slay him. But the Saint covered them with darkness, and when the Magi and the Druids beheld his power their hearts failed, and they bade the King cease his efforts, for that "a fire was that day kindled in Erin that would never be extinguished."

Afterwards Patrick and his band of followers appeared suddenly in the midst of the King's Court, and the Queen, struck with fear and terror by his preaching, was at once converted. It was at this time, also, that Patrick composed that wonderful hymn which still holds its place in Irish literature, unequaled for strength and simple grandeur. In this he prays against 'the spells of women, smiths, and Druids,' and invokes, in fine resonant words:

> "The power of God to guide me,
> The wisdom of God to teach me,
> The eye of God to watch over me,
> The ear of God to hear me,
> The shield of God to defend me."

For this hymn Patrick is described by Sechnall, one of his disciples, as 'the flame of a splendid sun, a stream of wisdom with splendor;' and he calls the hymn 'a diadem of princes, chanted music, a noble solace for men.' Further, it was on this memorable occasion that, in the presence of the King, and Queen, and Court, Patrick, taking the shamrock in his hand, addressed the people and taught them the mystery of the Trinity from the triune leaf, which has since been the national symbol of Ireland for a thousand years. But the Saint not only gave religion but culture to Ireland, for wherever he went he established schools, churches, and monasteries, where the Latin letters and alphabet were taught to the people, who before that had only the Ogham writing; and after this time Greek and Latin were freely taught in the Irish schools, and Latin became the ordinary tongue among the men of letters and learning. Thus, under his powerful guidance, the conversion of Ireland proceeded rapidly. Kings, queens, princes, chiefs and nobles, bards and Druids, were all brought into the fold, and before his death the conquest over paganism was complete. For his mode of action was full of tact; he did not overthrow the pagan rites, but converted them to

Christian usages. Thus, Beltaine, or the day of the Baal fire, became sacred as the Easter festival, and Samhain, the day of the dead and of demons, became Hallow Eve, the Day of Saints.

Patrick also confirmed the Brehon laws in so far as they were just, and upheld the privileges of the bard, he himself being a poet, at the same time giving honor to the priesthood above all. Thus, the bard was allowed seven colors in his raiment; but Patrick permitted eight colors in the sacred satin robe worn by the priest at the sacrament. This was called 'the robe of offering.' And before his time only three had the right to speak in public- namely, the historian, the poet, and the judge- but Patrick added another, 'the man of the lasting language'- that is, the priest of the Holy Canon. Learning he upheld in. high honor, and he himself taught the Latin letters to the converts. So that form of writing spread rapidly, and has remained in use ever since as the Irish alphabet.

The scribe, or man of letters, was esteemed a personage of such importance that whoever shed his blood was liable to the penalty of death, or obliged to pay a forfeit of seven slave girls, each girl being value three cows. But the Saint was cruel and remorseless against sin. His fair young sister Lupait angered him because she broke her vows and gave herself to her lover; on which Patrick cursed her and her lover Colmain, and vowed to keep them out of heaven. Then Lupait went forth to meet Patrick in the way as he drove in his chariot, and fell down on her knees before him, praying for mercy and that he would not take heaven away from her lover and their son Aedan. But Patrick sternly bade the charioteer to drive over her. Yet still she prayed for grace, and three times she ran in front of the chariot, and, kneeling down, entreated pardon and forgiveness. Then Patrick at last promised his sister that as she repented he would not take away heaven from her, yet that she must surely die; and again be bade the charioteer to drive on. So the third time the chariot passed over Lupait, and she lay dead before him in the path. Then Patrick had the Requiem sung, and she was buried as she died, in the place where the cross now stands; but her soul was suffered to enter heaven.

A softer and gentler spirit is in the story of the two princesses converted to the Christian faith by the Sanctus Patricius Episcopalus. One day the two daughters of the King of Meath, Ethna and Pedalma, on going down to the river to bathe, beheld St. Patrick and his converts all draped in flowing white robes, for they were celebrating morning prayers; and the princesses thought they must be of the fairy race (the Daine Sidhe), and they questioned them, on which Patrick expounded the Christian truth to them. And the maidens asked him many questions. "Who is your God? Is he young? Is he handsome? Has he sons and daughters? Are his daughters as handsome as we are? Is he rich? Is he young or aged? Is he to die like us, or does he live forever?" Then Patrick having satisfied them on all those points, the two maidens, Bthna and Fedalma, were baptized, and became zealous workers for the Christian cause at their father's royal Court of Tara of the Kings. St. Patrick was a great favorite with the Lord, and He sent His angel to him. to ask what things he desired most to be granted to him. On which the Saint made seven requests, among others, that no Outlander should ever rule over Ireland; that he, Patrick, should alone judge the Irish at the last day, even as the twelve who were deputed to judge Israel; and that every Thursday and Saturday twelve souls of the Irish people should be freed from the pains of hell.

It is interesting to reflect on the permanence of symbols and memories when once they have taken root in the heart of a nation. A thousand years may have passed by, yet still on the Saint's day every child in Ireland will wear a Patrick's cross on the shoulder, made in the national color, of green ribbon, and every Irishman throughout the world will be known by the shamrock in his hat, and every Irishwoman will have her bouquet of the Seamrogleanne, while to many an Irish exile in foreign lands the verdant and sacred symbol, fresh from the native sod, will be carefully sent by post as the most acceptable of presents, and at night there will be the great annual ball at Dublin Castle, in St. Patrick's Hall, when the Lord Lieutenant and all his suite will wear huge bunches of the national emblem, and all the ladies will have it mingled with their garlands and in the adornments of their dress.

Even a Royal levee will be held in London in the Saint's honor, where princes and peers will appear with the glittering insignia of the Order of St. Patrick; a special compliment to Ireland, for there is no Leek day, nor Thistle day, recognized in Court ceremonials. And no doubt the day of the festival will be fine, for St. Patrick made this a particular point with the angel sent to him to know his wishes, that on his special day, the 17th of March, no rain should fall; but the weather always be bright and fair, to allow the attendance of the faithful at the service of the Church.

And thus it has been for fourteen hundred years, for from that time till now no rain has fallen upon the Saint's day throughout the length and breadth of green Erin, no matter what may happen in the less favored regions of the earth outside the pale of 'Holy Ireland' the Insula Sanctorum, blessed for evermore by the great apostle, Saint, and guardian of the Irish race, whose sacred symbol we all wear in his honor.

A Legend of St. Patrick

One day three young princes came to Tara, where Patrick had erected his altar, and fell prostrate before the holy Saint, weeping bitterly. And they told him how they had fled away from the Court of the King because, in his anger, he had vowed to slay them with the sword unless they gave up their new religion and prayed again to the ancient idols; for they had become converts to the faith of Christ and worshiped only the God of the holy Patrick.

And their tears fell fast in the dust at the Saint's feet as they told their story, and said they were ready and willing to give up life itself, but never their faith in the one true God, whom they had learned to know from Patrick's teaching. Then the Saint being greatly moved with pity and tenderness, laid his finger on the cheek of each youth as the tears fell, and lo! the tears changed to pearls. "Now, swallow them," said the Saint, "and three sons will be born of you whose destiny is to overthrow the idolatries and the devil-worship of Erin."

And so it happened, for one of the sons born afterwards was the renowned St. Columba, the glory of the Church, and the light of Ireland and of the world.

St. Patrick and the Witch

When Patrick came over to Ireland to convert the pagans, no one would give him a lodging, for so the Druid priests had ordered. And he wandered on till at last he came to a small inn, where he was allowed to rest, the people not knowing him. And in the night he was thirsty, and asked for water; but the mistress told him she had forgotten to fill the vessels and there was no water except at the well, and not one of her servants or people would venture to go there at such an hour, so he must just bear the thirst on him till morning; for there was no use fighting the devil, and never a one ever came back from the well if they tried to brave him. Then Patrick said he would go himself and fill the can, and fetch it home. On this the woman wondered greatly, and asked what country he came from to be so brave, for a great enchanter lived by the well, and no one dared to go near it in the dark night. The Saint, however, made answer that he feared no harm, for God and the angels would guard him. So she gave him a wooden noggin with a lid to carry the water, and bade him take care how he lifted his eyes to look at the light set on the rock where the enchanter dwelt, or he would certainly fall down dazed and die. But Patrick, nothing fearing, went forth; and when he came to the rock by the well, he cast a strong spell over the place in the name of the Trinity, and the magician trembled and uttered a loud cry, and then dropped down dead on his face and spake no word.

So Patrick was at peace to fill the vessel with water from the well, and he returned safe to the inn. And it was a saying afterwards among the Irish, if they were offended or suffered injury, "The curse of St. Patrick on the man of the well be on your head for evermore!"

Now, the magician had a mother- a wicked witch called Churana- and she vowed vengeance on Patrick, and turned her sorceries against him. So he pursued her to Croagh-Patrick, where she lived, and ascended the mountain after her, though she flung down great rocks on him to stop his way. But he prayed to the Lord, who gave him strength to fling them aside, and still he went on up the mountain. Then the witch caused a great fog to arise, and he was left alone, for none of his disciples could find their way to follow him in the darkness. Still Patrick went on all alone, until, by chance, his foot struck against a bell on the mountain path ; and when he rang it, his followers heard and came to him. And. at last they gained the top, though all was black darkness around them by reason of the fog. And it was the first Sunday in harvest-time, which Sunday was called ever after through all the years Donagh-tram-dubh ('the Sunday of Gloom'). Then they began to descend the mountain. But the witch caused water to be poured over them that was nauseous to the smell and taste; so the Sunday is also called 'Garlic Sunday' ever since. Still, never heeding, they pursued her even as far as the great lake, where the evil witch plunged into the water. But Patrick struck her with the bell as she passed him and slew her; and her blood changed that water to red, so that the lake was known ever after as Lough-Dearg, or the 'Red Lake.'

And Patrick, in memory of his deliverance, established a station there and founded a monastery. And yet once more he ascended Croagh-Patrick, and beheld all the country lying westward; but, finding that his time was short, and that he could not visit Connemara nor the lands near, he lifted up his hands and invoked a blessing on the bays, and the harbors, and the shores of Connemara, even a seven-fold blessing. So ever since the fish are abundant there beyond all other places on the coast of Ireland. Nor yet had he time to visit Erris; but, unhappily, he forgot, before leaving the mountain, to invoke a blessing on the island, so the people of Erris are still pagan in all their ways- rakish and prodigal, and given to strong drink, even to this clay- for the blessing of Patrick never rested on them, nor on their land or coasts.

FESTIVALS

May Day in Ireland

Every race since Creation has tried to express man's intuitive belief in the invisible world by some visible image, or occult symbol, or mystic legend; and thus the primitive traditions of humanity have been faithfully preserved as a sacred ritual that it would be fatal to disregard. In Ireland the ancient usages are still adhered to as firmly as they were three thousand years ago, when they expressed a religion, and the gods of the people were the visible forces of nature. The awakening of spring to life and beauty, after the death-sleep of winter, especially touched the human heart with joy and hope, and was celebrated with garlands, and music, and song. Mystic symbols were fashioned to represent the mysteries of nature, and strange mystic stories of the rush of spirit-life through the world were repeated by every successive generation till they became indelibly stamped on the national heart and memory. They are still recited at the popular festivals by the professional village bards, and crooned over by the old women at the wakes and christenings, or told with awful solemnity to the listening children as they crouch round the turf fire of a winter's night, eager to hear the weird stories of witches and demons; of the dead who walk in their white shrouds on certain nights, when to meet them is fatal to the living; or of the mysterious fairy race, the fallen angels of heaven, who have been cast down to earth to expiate their sins, and who live in crystal caves paved with gold beneath the sea, or in the mountain clefts, where the caverns are lit by the diamonds that stud the rocks, and who sip nectar from the cups of the flowers, and weave their gossamer robes of the sunbeam and the glittering dewdrops. And many a pretty girl, as she listens, longs to dance in the moonlight with these fairy beings under the scented hawthorn tree, for the Sidhe (the fairies) are more beautiful and graceful than any of the children of earth, though a deep sorrow rests ever on them, knowing that at the last day they are destined to eternal death, while the human race will live in heaven forevermore.

A number of ancient traditions circle especially round May Day, called in Irish La-Bel-Taine (the day of the sacred 'Baal-fire'), because in the old pagan times, on May Eve, the Druids lit the great sacred fire at Tara, and as the signal flames rose up high in the air, a fire was kindled on every hill in Erin, till the whole island was circled by a zone of flame. It is a saying among the Irish, "Fire and salt are the two most precious things given to man." Fire, above all, was held sacred by them, as the symbol of Deity and the mystic means of purification, and three things were never given away by them on May Day- fire, milk, or butter for this would be to give away luck. No one was permitted to carry a lighted sod out of the house, or to borrow fire in any way. And no strange hand was allowed to milk the cow, for if the first can were filled in the name of the devil there would be no more milk that year for the family- it would all be secretly taken away by the fairies.

The first three days of May were very dangerous to cattle, for the fairies had then great power given them of the Evil One; therefore they were well guarded by lighted fires and branches of the rowan, and the milkmaid made the sign of the Cross after milking, with the froth of the milk. Nothing else was so effective against witches and demons. During the first three days of May, also, it was necessary to take great precautions against the fairies entering the house, for if once they gained admittance they worked mischief. They would come disguised as old women or wayfarers in order to steal a burning coal- a most fatal theft- or to carry off the herbs of power, that were always gathered on May morning with the dew on them. But the best preventive against fairy or demon power was to scatter primroses on the threshold, for no fairy could pass the flower, and the house and household were left in peace, though all strangers were looked upon with great suspicion. A young student was nearly killed one time by the people, for they saw him walking up and down on May morning on the grass, while he read aloud from a book in some strange language; and they concluded that he was trying to bewitch the herbs of grace, which are for healing. Fortunately, however, a priest came by, and having examined the book, found it was a copy of Virgil; so he informed the excited crowd that the young man was simply going through his college duties in the grand old language that St. Patrick had brought to Ireland, and which was sacred forever to the use of the Church. On this they were pacified, and the young student was allowed to depart in safety.

A curious superstition is still prevalent among the people

that on May Day the ancient kings of Ireland arise from their graves and gather together a great army of the dead, horse and foot, and they tell the troops that the hour has come to fight for Ireland, and they must be ready to march as commanded. Then the spectral warriors clash their shields and respond with wild cries to the kings and chiefs and captains of the nation. The last time the kings arose from their graves was, it is said, in 1848, when the tramp and the shouts of the marching men resounded distinctly through the hills; but when the people rushed to the spot where the shields clashed and the voices sounded, not a form was visible; the hosts of the dead warriors had vanished into air. Many of the old customs still remain among the peasants. Among others it is thought right and proper to have the threshold swept clean on May Eve. Ashes are then lightly sprinkled over it, and in the morning the print of a foot is looked for. If it turn inward a marriage is certain, but if outward then a death will happen in the family before the year is out. The cattle also are still singed along the back with a lighted wisp of straw, and a bunch of primroses is tied to the cow's tail, for the evil spirits cannot touch anything guarded by these flowers, if they are plucked before sunrise, not else. But the rowan tree is the best preservative against evil; if a branch be woven into the roof, the house is safe for a year at least, and if mixed with the timber of a boat no storm will upset it, and no man be drowned in it for the next twelvemonth.

May Day in old time was the period of greatest rejoicing in Ireland, a festival of dances and garlands to celebrate the Resurrection of Nature, as November was a time of solemn gloom and mourning for the dying sun; for the year was divided into these two epochs, symbolizing death and resurrection, and the year itself was expressed by a word meaning 'the circle of the sun,' the symbol of which was a hoop, always carried in the popular processions, wreathed with the rowan and the marsh marigold, and bearing, suspended within it, two balls to represent the sun and moon, sometimes covered with gold and silver paper. This emblem of the hoop and the balls is still carried on May Day by the villagers, though the meaning has been lost when it was consecrated to Baal, according to the solemn oath of the Irish, 'by the sun, moon, stars, and wind.' At the great long dance held on May Day all the people held hands and danced round a tall May bush erected on a mound, the girls wearing garlands, while the pipers and harpers, with gold and green sashes, directed the movements. The oldest worship of the world included homage to the tree and the serpent. Trees were the symbol of knowledge, and the dance round the May bush, which simulated the sinuous curves of the serpent, was part of the ancient ophite ritual associated with the worship of Baal. The dance and the May bush still exist, but the fairy music seems to be lost forever. In the ancient days it was heard upon May Eve on all the hills of Erin, and the most beautiful tunes were thus caught up by the people and the native musicians. Carolan, it is said, the celebrated bard, acquired all the magic melody of his notes by sleeping out on a fairy rath at night, when the fairy music came to him in dreams, and on awaking he played the airs from memory; but since his time the fairies seem to keep silence on the hills, and no more exquisite airs have been added to the pathetic national music of Ireland.

The educated and learned are as susceptible to the mysterious prescience of an invisible spiritual world as the illiterate Irish peasant. Every one is conscious of the strange influence upon life of omens and dreams, and of days when the malefic powers, whose mission seems to be to torture the human race, are fearful and strong, and ruthlessly crush all our wishes and resolves, showing us how weak and powerless we are to order life as we desire, or to gain control over even the simplest events; of days when all things are fatally unlucky; of the presence of certain persons who chill the heart and stifle the eloquence of the lips; or of others who pour a warm flood of genius into the veins and make us divine for the moment that we are under their magic spell. So we may sympathize with the Irish peasant, who has given definite forms to the superstitions that we only dimly feel, and recognize the kinship of all races and classes by the universal intuition, common to all humanity, of a mysterious, unseen world of spiritual beings around us. These are for ever influencing our actions or directing our destiny, though we cannot hear them playing their sweet music on the hills, or see them dancing under the scented hawthorn, like the Irish peasant, who watches the Baal fires on the mountains flaming up through the midnight to announce the coming of May.

The fairies exercise a very powerful influence for evil at Bel-Taine, or May time; so as a preservative against their malice and the fairy darts, which at this season wound and kill, it is the custom on May morning, at sunrise, to bleed the cattle and taste of the blood mingled with milk. Men and women were also bled, and their blood was sprinkled on the ground. This practice, however, has died out, even in the remote West; but the children are still lifted through the fire when it has burned low, and the cattle are driven through the hot embers- as in ancient times both children and cattle were 'passed through the fire to Moloch'- and the young men still leap through the flames after the dance round the burning bush is over, and they carry home a lighted branch of the sacred tree to give good luck to the family during the coming year. May Day in pagan Ireland was the great festival of Baal, or Grian, the Sun. Then the fires were lighted on the Druid altars, and the great sacrifice of the year was offered. November, the month of gloom, was also sacred to the Sun, when the fires were lighted to guide him in his descent to the kingdom of death; and at both seasons the sacrifices and ceremonies were made sacred through fire, the great symbol of the creative, all-sustaining God, and the source of all life through the universe.

The origin of the May bush, or burning tree, was thus described by an intelligent peasant, who had it from his father, an old man about eighty years of age, well versed in the old traditions of the people: "The lighted May bushes," the old man said unto me, "were first set up in honor of the great Milesians, who gave battle on May Day to the Tuatha de Danans, and conquered. Then a powerful magician of the Tuatha caused innumerable fiery darts to go forth against the Prince of the Milesians to kill him; but, in passing, they were all stopped by a bush that stood between the chief and the magician, so that a flame arose, and the bush withered and burned away. And from that time the May bushes are lit by fire and left to burn, for so evil is carried away from the land; and we believe and know that no lightning, nor thunder, nor evil enchantments can ever enter a house before which stands the sacred bush with the yellow flowers that represent the flame of fire; and the people dance round it, and pass their cattle through the smoke, with also the young children, to preserve them from the spell of witchcraft."

This was the story told by the peasant, as he heard it through the traditions of his father.

The May-Day Dance

Dancing was the most important of the sacred rites in all ancient religions; and the circular serpent-dance round the tree has been practiced from the remotest antiquity. In Ireland it is still retained as the favorite pastime of the people on the La-Bel-Taine (May Day), when all the young men and maidens hold hands, and dance in a circle round a tree hung with ribbons and garlands, or round a bonfire, moving in curves from right to left, as if imitating the windings of a serpent, though quite unconscious of the cryptic meaning of the movement, which is, in reality, a true ophite hieroglyph of the earliest traditions of humanity concerning the serpent and the tree.

ANCIENT CURES, CHARMS, AND USAGES OF IRELAND

Advice to Maidens

On May morning, before sunrise, go out to the garden, and the first snail you see take up, and put it on a plate sprinkled lightly with flour, place a cabbage-leaf over, and so leave it till after sunrise, when yon will find the initial letters of your lover's name traced on the flour. Should the snail be quite within his house when you take him up, your lover will be rich; but should the snail be almost out of his shell, then your future husband will be poor, and probably will have no house or home to take you to when you wed him. Therefore take good heed of the warning given to you by the snail, or avoid trying your future fate if you are afraid of the result.

May Eve

Great precautions must be taken on May Eve, for the fairies have fatal power over the human race upon that night, and steal the children and bewitch the cattle if they can find an opportunity; therefore no door should be left open after sunset, and young persons should not go out alone on the hills, nor listen to the singing of young girls in the night, for they are fairies in disguise, and will work harm. And, above all, fire, should not be given away, for fire is the life of man; and if any food, boiled, roast, or baked, is left over from May Eve to May Day, it must not be eaten, but buried in the garden, or thrown over the boundary of the town-land for the dogs, because the fairies stole away the real food at night, and left in its place only lumps of turf sod, made to look like food, and to touch them would be fatal.

May-Day Usages

On May morning the peasant girls delight in gathering

May dew before sunrise, to beautify their faces, and they believe that the sun will then have no power over their complexions to spoil them by the summer heat ; and no fire is lighted in any home until the smoke is seen rising from the chimney of the priest's house, which, to the modern world, is like the first fire on the Druid altar of old, that gave the signal of the uprising of the Sun-God.

Whitsuntide

Whitsuntide has always been considered by the Irish as a very fatal and unlucky time- for the people hold that fairies and evil spirits have then great power over men and cattle, both by sea and land, and work their deadly spells with malign and mysterious efficacy. Children born at Whitsuntide, it is said, are foredoomed; they will either have the evil eye, or commit a murder, or die a violent death. Water, also, is very dangerous; no one should bathe, or go a journey where a stream has to be crossed, or sail in a boat, for the risk is great of being drowned, unless, indeed, a bride steers, and then the boat is safe from harm. Great precautions are necessary, likewise, within the house; and no one should venture to light a candle without making the sign of the Cross over the flame to keep off evil; and young men should be very cautious not to be out late at night, for all the dead who have been drowned in the sea round about come up and ride over the waves on white horses, and hold strange revels, and try to carry off the young men, or to kill them with their fiery darts and draw them down under the sea to live with the dead forevermore. A story is told of a man named Murrey, who stayed out late fishing one Whitsuntide, quite forgetting it was the night of the death-ride.

But at last he neared the shore, and drew up his boat to unload the fish, and then make his way home with all speed. Just at the moment, however, he heard a great rush of the waves behind him, and looking round he saw a crowd of the dead on their white horses making over to the boat to seize him; and their faces were pale as the face of a corpse, but their eyes burned like fire. And they stretched out their long skeleton arms to try and lay hold of him, but he sprang at once from the boat to the shore, and then he knew he was safe, though one of them rode over close to him by the edge of the rocks, and he knew him as a friend of his own, who had been drowned the year before; and he heard the voice of the dead man calling to him through the rush of water, saying: "Hasten, hasten to your home, for the dead who are with me want you for their company, and if once a dead hand touches you, there is no help, you are lost for ever. Hasten, or you will never see your home again, but be with the dead forever." Then Murrey knew that the spirit spoke the truth, and he left the boat and the fish on the beach and fled away home, and never looked back at the dead on their white horses, for his heart was filled with. fear. And never again did he go out to fish at Whitsuntide, though the dead waited for him to seize him, but he came not, and lived henceforth safe from harm. At this season, also, the fairy queens make great efforts to carry off the fine stalwart young men of the country to the fairy palace in the cleft of the hills, or to lure them to their dancing grounds, where they are lulled into dreams by the sweet, subtle fairy music, and forget home and kith and kindred, and never desire to return again to their own people; or even if the spell is broken, and they are brought back by some strong incantation, yet they are never the same, for everyone knows by the dream-look in their eyes that they have danced with the fairies on the hill, and been loved by one of the beautiful but fatal race, who, when they take a fancy to a handsome mortal lover, cast their spells over him with resistless power.

A case of this kind happened some years ago in the County Wexford. Two brothers, fine young fellows of the farming class, were returning home one evening in Whitsuntide from their day's holiday, when, to their surprise, as they crossed a broad, beautiful field, lit up by the red rays of the setting sun, they saw a group of girls dancing, and they were all draped in white, and their long hair fell floating over their shoulders. So lovely was the sight that the young men could not choose but stop and watch the dancers; yet, strange to say, they were all strangers; not a familiar face was among them from the whole country round.

And as they looked and wondered, one of the girls left the dance, and, coming over to the younger brother, laid her hand on his arm, while she murmured softly in his ear: "Come, dance with me, Brian. I have waited long for you. Come, come!" and she drew him gently away. Then Brian flung down his stick on the ground, and taking her hand, they were soon whirling away in the dance, the handsomest pair that ever trod a measure on the green sod. Long, long they danced, till the red light passed away, and the darkness began to cover the hills, but still they danced on and on, for Brian heeded nothing save the young girl with her long hair floating on his shoulder, and the fire of her eyes that burned into his heart. At last the elder brother called to him, "Brian, come home; leave the dance; the mother will be waiting for us!", "Not yet, not yet," answered Brian; "I must finish this round. Leave me, and I will follow you." So the elder brother left, and he and the mother watched and waited till midnight for Brian's return, but he never came. Then, the next morning, the brother went to see after him, searching everywhere, though in vain. And all that day to sunset and the night he searched, still no tidings could be had. No one had seen him in the dance, nor the young girls with the white dresses and the floating hair, though when the neighbors heard the story they looked very solemn, and said there was no help for the doomed young man, for the fairy power was strong at Whitsuntide, and no doubt they had carried him down under the earth to the fairy palace, and he would never, never come back to his home again.

Then the poor mother fell into terrible grief, and she sent for the wisest fairy-doctor in the place, and asked his advice. Now, the old man came of a great race who had known the fairy secrets and the mysteries through many generations, though they kept the knowledge to themselves, and would tell no one how they gained power over fairies and demons. "Well, now, my good woman," he said, "the fairies have your son, for the daughter of the great fairy chief loves him, and will not let him go. And if he has eaten their food or drunk of their wine no one can help him, not even I myself, until a year has passed by. But next Whitsuntide, when the fairies come for their mad revels and dances out of the heart of the mountains and up from the depths of the sea, they will bring your son with them, and if my power can reach him he will be free from this witchcraft, and the spell shall be broken. So let his brother go and meet him in the same field at the same hour, and there he will find him dancing in the sunset with his fairy bride; or go yourself, if you are alive, and I will give you a spell and a charm that has power to break the strongest fairy thrall." So when Whitsuntide came round, the elder brother set out on his search, and there, sure enough, in the very same green field, with the red sunset streaming down, was the group of young girls in their white dresses dancing to the music of the fairy pipes; and in the midst was Brian, dancing with his fairy bride, and her long yellow hair floated over his shoulder, and her eyes burned into his like coals of fire.

"Come away, come away, Brian," cried the brother; "you have been dancing long enough, and the mother is at home, sad, and sorrowful, and lonely, waiting for you. Come away, before the darkness falls and the night comes on.", "Not yet, not yet," answered Brian; "I must finish this dance." And the fairy bride wound her beautiful white arms round him and held him fast. So the brother lost heart, for he feared to enter the circle lest the enchantment should fall on him; and he went back home to tell of his failure.

Then the mother rose up, and taking the charm which the fairy-man had given her, she hung it round her neck and went forth to look for the missing son. And at last she came to the field and saw him dancing and dancing like mad, with the witch-girl in his arms; and she called to him, "Come back, come back to us, Brian darling, come back; it is your mother calls." But Brian danced on and on, and never looked at her nor heeded her. Then, for the sorrow made her brave, she went over in the very midst of the fairy dancers with their glittering eyes, and taking the spell from her neck, she flung it over Brian, and clasping his arm laid her head down on his shoulder, weeping bitterly. Then, all at once, the demon spell was broken, for a mother's tears have strange power, and he let her take his hand and draw him away from the magic circle; and the form of the fairy bride seemed to melt into the sunset, and the whole scene passed away like a mist, the music and the dancers with their floating hair, and only Brian and his mother were left in the field. Then she led him home, but he spake no word, only lay down to sleep, and so for seven days they watched by him, but still he slept. Then at the end of the seven days he rose up strong and well as ever, and all the past seemed to him only as a dream. Yet, for fear of the fairies, his mother still made him wear the magic spell round his neck to keep him from harm, though in process of time a still stronger spell was woven round his life, for he married a fair young girl of the village before the next Whitsuntide, good as well as beautiful, and from that time the fairies and witches had no more power over him, for a pure, true wife is the best safeguard against witchcraft and devils' wiles that a man can take to his heart as the angel of the house.

Hallowtide in Ireland

The ancient Irish had two great divisions of the year, Samradh and Geimradh- summer and winter- corresponding to the May and November of our calendar; one represented the resurrection of nature and all things to life, the other the descent of all things to darkness and death. La-samnah, or Hallow Eve, was considered the summer end, the first day of winter, when the Sun-God entered the kingdom of death; therefore, on that night of gloom the great sacred fire was lighted on every Druid altar to guide him on his downward path; and the Druid priests sacrificed a black sheep, and offered libations to the dead who had died within the year.

It was a weird season of dread and ill omen, and for this reason November was called by the Irish 'the month of mourning' Then it was that Baal, the lord of death, summoned before him the souls of the dead to receive judgment for the works done in the human life; and on the vigil of Saman, or Hallow Eve, the dead had strange power over the living, and could work them harm, and take revenge for any wrong done to them while they lived. Even now, according to the popular belief, it is not safe to be near a churchyard on Hallow Eve, and people should not leave their homes after dark, or the ghosts would pursue them. For on that one night of the year power is given to the dead, and they rise from their graves and go forth amid the living, and can work good or evil, no man hindering; and at midnight they hold a festival like the fairies of the hill, and drink red wine from fairy cups, and dance in their white shrouds to fairy music till the first red dawn of day. For Hallow Eve is the great festival of the dead, when their bonds are loosed, and they revel with mad joy in the life of the living. And if on that night you hear footsteps following you, beware of looking round; it is the dead who are behind you; and if you meet their glance, assuredly you must die.

The first day of November was dedicated to the spirit that presides over fruits and seeds, and was called La-mas-abhal, the day of the apple fruit; but this being pronounced Lamabool, the English settlers corrupted the word into lamb's-wool, which name they gave to a strong composition made of apples, sugar, and ale. So on this night in every house the table was piled with apples and the gathering of the nut trees, and handfuls of nuts were flung into the fire by the young people to burn; for it was believed that strange and startling prognostications of fate and future fortune could be made from tie ashes. Many weird and fearful rites were also practiced at this season to obtain a knowledge of the future, for all incantations at Hallowtide were made in the name of the Evil One; and this solemn and gloomy ritual of death and sorcery lasted through the entire month of November, until a prophecy of hope, as it were, arose with December, called by the Irish Mi-Nolagh, 'the month of the new-born.'

The number two is esteemed the most unlucky of all numbers; therefore the second day of November was appointed for the sacrifice to the dead, and certain incantations were used to bring up the spirits from the grave and compel them to answer questions. But for this purpose blood must be spilled, for it is said the spirits love blood; the color excites them, and gives them for the moment the sensation of life. However, during the incantations, very strange and fatal results sometimes happened to the questioner. On one occasion a dead man in his shroud answered the call, and drew away the girl who had performed the rite from the midst of the people assembled; but the fright turned her brain, and she never afterwards recovered her reason.

On the Vigil of Saman, or Hallow Eve, the peasants of Ireland used to assemble with sticks and clubs, the ancient emblems of laceration, and go about collecting barley cakes, butter, eggs, meal, and all things necessary for a feast; likewise money to purchase the black sheep, so important for the sacrifice. After this candles were lighted, before which they prayed for the souls of the dead, and at midnight the unholy practices began, from which the young men and maidens tried to learn the secrets of the future. Then the hemp seed was sown in the name of the Evil One, and the girls would hang a garment before the fire, and watch from a corner to see the shadowy apparition of the destined husband come down the chimney to turn it; and a ball of yarn was flung from the window, when the apparition would appear below and wind the yarn, while the Paternoster was recited backwards.

But the incantation before the looking-glass was the most fearful of all, for the face of the future husband would appear in the glass, though sometimes a form filled up the surface of the mirror too terrible to describe. A young girl once practiced this evil rite all alone in her room, the door being closed. After some time a violent scream was heard, and when her friends rushed in to the rescue they found her fainting with terror. Yet she kept silent, and would reveal nothing, and next night she announced her intention to repeat the spell all alone, with closed door. They tried to dissuade her, but in vain. Alone she entered the room, and a profound silence followed. Her friends thought no danger was to be feared, and they were jesting and laughing when a terrible shriek resounded from the apartment, and on entering they found the girl lying dead upon the floor, her features horribly contorted, while the looking-glass was shivered to atoms.

Another practice is to carry the looking-glass outside, and let the rays of the moon fall on the surface, when a face will be revealed, connected for good or evil with the future fate of the holder of the mirror. The young girls also visit the neighboring gardens at night, blindfold, to tear up cabbages by the root. If the one first seized is a close, white cabbage, an old man is the destined husband; but if an open, green head, then a young lover may be hoped for. Another custom is to make a cake of yellow clay taken from a churchyard, then stick twelve pieces of candle in it, and, kneeling down, recite a form of witch-prayer while all the candles are lighted, and a name is given to each one of them. According as the lights burn out, so will the fate be of the person whose name it bears, and the first that is extinguished betokens death. To obtain a knowledge of the future is the object of all the strange and mystic rites practiced at Hallowtide. The young girls sometimes rake out the ashes of the fire overnight, making a. perfectly flat surface on the hearth. This is done in the name of the Evil One, and the result is sure to come in a certain and fatal sign, for in the morning the print of a foot will be found distinctly marked in the ashes. If the impress is perfectly flat, it indicates marriage and a long life; but if the toes are bent down into the ashes, death will inevitably follow.

They also make a cake of flour, mixed with soot and a spoonful of salt, bake it, and eat it. It will cause thirst, and if a man offers a drink at the time, the girl will assuredly be married before the year is out. The young men seeking brides have other forms of incantation. If a man on Hallow Eve creeps under the long, trailing branches of the briar on which blackberries grow, he will see the shadow of the girl he is to marry; but he must first pronounce some words too awful to be written down, for they come of the Evil Spirit's teaching. And if a gambler hides under the tendrils of the briar, and invokes the aid of the Prince of Darkness, he will have luck at cards, no matter what color he bets on. But the words he uses are too diabolical to repeat; only a witch-woman can utter them, and she whispers the spell into the ears of the man at dead of night, none hearing her.

From old times in Ireland the people attached great importance to the grave-clothes in which one they love is buried; for a belief is prevalent that the dead continue to wear the clothes they last used in this world whenever they may have occasion, to appear on earth. It is, therefore, considered very lucky for the dead person to have a new or a good suit of clothes in his possession at the time of death, for then he will always appear respectable when he goes among the other ghosts, as they rise from their graves and meet together on the night of the festival of the dead. The nearest relation may wear the clothes in the daytime, but at night the dead come back and require them, should they have any work to do in the neighborhood of the churchyard. For this reason no alteration in size is permitted of the death garments, as the ghost would be exceedingly angry if, by any such practice on the part of the relations, the clothes proved to be a misfit, just, perhaps, at the very time when he wanted to begin his midnight rambles amid the living on the solemn and awful November festival.

If possible, therefore, the people procure a religious habit for the burial, as this distinction, they know, will be esteemed a high compliment by the dead, and give them dignity among the other ghosts. Thus, is is told that a poor woman having lost her only son,, expended all her hoarded savings on the purchase of a habit for his burial, and in this he was laid in the grave; yet night after night for a week her son appeared to her in dreams, looking unutterably sad, though he spake no word.

On this the mother became much troubled in her mind, and prayed the Lord God to show her in what way she had failed in her duty as regarded the burial rites. So the next night in her dream she saw her son again, and he came over quite close to her bed, and looking at her with hollow, mournful eyes, said, "Look here, my mother, do you not see how all my legs are scorched in purgatory, because the habit you gave me is too short, and only comes down to the knees? So unless you can add a good piece to lengthen it, my legs will be burned off entirely before ever I come before the angels in heaven; and as to going out with the other ghosts for the festival, why, they would only mock at me. Help me, then, my mother, before it is too late." And with that he departed; but the poor mother heeded his words, and next day she had the coffin raised and opened, and with her, own hands she sewed a good piece of stuff all round the habit to lengthen it and make it proper and right. Then the coffin was closed and laid in the earth again, and after that the mother was troubled no more with dreams, for the dead rested quiet in the grave, and the soul was at peace.

Among the most solemn of the adepts who practiced weird and mystical charms at Hallowtide, and recited prayers to the Evil One, to give them a knowledge of the future, there was a certain class who followed the strictest rules of living, and abstained entirely from the stimulating poteen during the performance of their incantations; but others, who desired power over demons and evil spirits, worked up their energies to a species of delirium by copious draughts of the national beverage, which they considered a potent strengthener of the organs of the body, and powerful to give courage to the heart of a man if properly taken with honey and bread, so as prevent harm to the liver or the brain, according to the advice of the native doctors.

The English settlers were not slow to recognize the merits of poteen, and Richard Stanihurst, in his description of Ireland, thus eulogizes the Irish stimulant:

"Being moderately taken, its sloweth age, it strengtheneth youth, it helpeth digestion, it cutteth phlegm, it abandoneth melancholy, it relisheth the heart, it lighteneth the mind, it quickeneth the spirit, it cureth hydropsis, it pounceth the stone, it keepeth the head from whirling, the eyes from dazzling, the tongue from lisping, the mouth from maffling, the teeth from chattering, and the throat from rattling. It keepeth the weason from stifling, the stomach from wambling, the heart from swelling, the hands from shivering, and the sinews from shrinking, the veins from crumbling, the bones from aching, and the marrow from softening."

ANCIENT CURES, CHARMS, AND USAGES OF IRELAND

This hymn to poteen shows the genial spirit in which Irish ideas were received and assimilated in former times by the English colonists, who thus became, according to the words of the chronicle, 'more Irish than the Irish themselves.' Such a stimulant was indeed necessary for the people at Hallowtide, when the air was filled with the presence of the dead, and everything around became a symbol or prophecy of fate. The name of a person called from the outside was a most dangerous omen; but if repeated three times, the result was fatal. Birds also came as messengers of fate during Hallowtide, and their appearance was generally a prognostication of evil. Once, at a great lord's house, a white pigeon came for three days in succession and perched on the window-sill, outside a room where the lady of the castle was laying ill. "Oh, my God!" she exclaimed, at last, "that white bird has come for me!" and the omen was fatally true; for before the week was out the young mother lay dead, with her baby beside her, and both were buried in the one coffin. But it is well to know that if a bird of ill omen should happen to come to the house, such as the raven or the water-wagtail, who is Satan's own emissary, the best way to turn aside the evil influence is to say at once: "Fire and water be on you, and in your mouth; and may the curse be on your head, bird of evil, forevermore."

And further, three candles must never be left lighted at once in the room. If these and other precautions are duly taken against evil spirits, then Hallowtide, or 'the month of gloom,' may pass over safely, without the fear of a dead hand being suddenly laid upon the shoulder, or words of doom being whispered in the ear by an unseen spirit, while the apples and nuts are piled upon the board for the ancient festival of La-mas-abhal.

ANCIENT CURES, CHARMS, AND USAGES OF IRELAND

Garland Sunday

(The first Sunday in September)

This was a great festival with the people from the most ancient times, and was devoted by the Irish to solemn rites in honor of their dead kindred. The garland, or hoop, was decorated the night before with colored ribbons, but the flowers that encircled it were not plucked till the morning of the great day, and only unmarried girls were allowed to gather the flowers and wreathe the garland, for the touch of a married woman's hand in the decorations was deemed unlucky. Then all the company proceeded to the churchyard, the finest young man in the village being chosen to carry the garland. From the topmost hoop some apples were suspended by their stalks, and if one dropped off during the procession, it was considered a lucky omen for the garland-bearer, a prophecy of long life and success in love; but if an apple fell after the garland was set up in the graveyard, it was looked on as a sign of ill luck and coming evil, especially to those who were dancing at the time; for a dance always closed the festival, after prayers were said, and flowers were strewn, with weeping and wailing, over the recent graves. The Irish nature passes lightly from sorrow to mirth, and the evening that began in tears ended in feasting and dances, while the garland of hospitality was offered to the mourning strangers, who had come, perhaps, a long distance to do honor to their dead kindred.

Sometimes a romance is interwoven with the ceremonial. A widow is seen superintending the making of the garland for her dead husband by the hands of her daughter, the pretty Eileen; while the girl's lover, the handsomest young fellow in the village, is selected to be the garland-bearer. Next day they join the procession to the churchyard, the widow and Eileen walking beside the young man. At times he shakes the pole bearing the garland, hoping to bring down an apple for luck, but none falls. Then the prayers are said, and the mourning is made round the garland, as they place it in the shadow of the old sacred ruin in the graveyard; after which a plank is laid for the dancing at the place where the garland is fixed, and all the youths and the garland maidens commence the dance. But Eileen will not join it, though her lover prays her to dance with him. Still she refuses, saying she must, stay with her mother while she prays. At last, however, she consents, and dances with her lover, looking radiant and happy; when suddenly two apples fall at their feet from the garland, but in the excitement of the dance the evil omen is scarcely heeded. A month after the young lovers were married, and the sign of coming evil was quite forgotten. Yet the evil came; for while out boating with some friends during the week of the marriage festivities, a storm suddenly came on, and the boat was upset. All, however, were saved, except the pretty bride and her handsome husband-lover, who were engulfed in the stormy waves, and seen no more; for the ancient signs of good and evil are true and certain, and no one can evade their destiny. As it is foretold, so it must come, be it for ban or blessing.

Peasant Games

There is a curious ancient game called 'The Game of the Rope,' which is still very popular, even at the present day, among the young people when assembled at a wake or a festival. The account of it may be best given in the words of a peasant artisan, who in his youth was often present at these wake ceremonies, and thus describes the game: "I am the son of a peasant, and was reared in the wildest part of Mayo, on the line of the mountains of Partry. There I learned the trade of a tailor, and had always plenty of work to do at home, besides being asked to all the villages round, whenever there was a wake, or wedding, or any other diversion going on. For the young men always wanted me at such times to make them smart and nice for the dances and fun. Slapping hands is the first game played at a wake, just while the company is coming in and sitting down. Then more regular games begin, when the handsomest girls are led out first, and the best partners are chosen for them. But 'The Game of the Rope' is the prime favorite after all.

Two short ropes, made of hay and twisted as hard as they can be made, are held by two men, standing at each side of a chair placed at some little distance from the corpse lying in the coffin. Then a young man is led forward, who takes his seat on the chair, and they ask him who is his sweetheart. If he objects to tell, they beat him till he names one of the girls present. Then he is asked would he like to kiss her, and they beat him till he answers yes. The girl is then led over and seated on the chair, while the lover kisses her; but as he is beaten all the time with the rope, he makes the ceremony as brief as possible.

The girl is then asked if she is content, and sometimes, for fun, she tells them that the lover they gave her had no idea of a proper kiss at all, on which the young man is beaten again with the ropes, till he cries out that he will try again. But the girl won't have him; and so the game goes on, till every young man in the room has been seated on the chair in succession, and every girl has been kissed. And so ends, with much laughter, 'The Game of the Rope.'"

Wake Games

There are also many^other wake games still in use among the people. A peasant who was familiar with these 'wake tricks,' as he called them, thus describes some of them:

"In the game of 'Shuffle the Brogue' twenty or thirty of the young people sit round on bundles of straw, forming a circle, all close together, the knees drawn up to the chin, and the feet pointing to the center. A young man then takes his place within the circle- generally a fine, active young fellow- and his office is to find the brogue and capture it as it is shuffled rapidly round the circle. Often during the search he gets many a blow on the back, and tries, unsuccessfully, to seize the assailant. But at length he is lucky enough to capture the brogue; and then he is asked to name his sweetheart, and permission is given to kiss her as his reward. But no girl is allowed to be kissed twice in the evening; it is enough to have been kissed once by her lover."

Another game is called 'The Horse Fair.' The leader or chief man, holding a brogue in his hand, ties a string of puny young men together as horses, and drives them round the circle, while another man goes in front and drags them on by the rope, striking any who are restive with the brogue. Then a blacksmith and a horse-dealer appear, and they examine the horses and put them through their paces. A short, stout young fellow is named the 'Cob,' another with long legs is the 'Race Horse,' a jolly young man is the 'Pony;' and after they are all tried, the horse-dealer declares he must see them jump before lie bids for them. So a great circle is made, a man being in the center, bent as in leap-frog, for them to leap over, while the young girls sit round, and the best jumper is allowed the privilege of choosing the maiden he likes best, and giving her a salute. The young horses generally succeed in the jump, th6 reward is so attractive, though two men are never allowed to kiss the same girl. Should one man fail in the jump, he is derided and beaten with brogues, and ordered to be sent for further training, and the smith is desired to see to his shoes. So he is laid flat on the ground, while the smith examines his shoes, and beats the sole of the foot with a big stick to see if a nail is loose and wants to be fastened; but then his sweetheart intervenes, and he is let off, and even allowed to salute her as a recompense for all he has gone through.

Another game is called 'The Mock Marriage.' Two clever

young wake-men dress themselves fantastically as priest and clerk, the latter carrying a linen bag filled with turf ashes, which he swings about to keep order, giving a good hit now and then, while the dust promotes a good deal of coughing among the crowd. But nothing irreverent is meant; for it is considered that whatever keeps up the spirits at a wake is allowable, and harmless in the sight of God. The priest then takes his place in the circle, the clerk at his elbow, and pours forth a volley of gibberish Latin, after which he calls out the names of those who are to be married, the selection being always most incongruous; and the clerk seizes them and hurries them forward, the bag of ashes enforcing obedience to the call.

As the names are called out, each man takes his place by the bride named for him, and the priest begins the ceremony in Irish, adding a homily, describing the horrid life probably reserved for the bride and bridegroom, owing to their vile temper and other bad qualities. But this is all pure fun, as nothing private or personal would be permitted. Then the clerk whirls his bag of ashes, and threatens to strike any man who grumbles at the wife he has got, and he demands his fee. Something must be given to him, a penny, or even a button, and the bride must give an article of her own property; but this is returned to her, and she is told they only wanted to test her obedience. After the ceremony is over, whiskey is served round, and priest and clerk and the bridegroom drink a glass for good luck, while the bride sips a little from her husband's glass.

No widow or widower, or married man or woman, is allowed to take part in this game, and nothing is said that could offend or lead to quarreling and fighting. Meantime, the corner of the room where the corpse lies in a coffin is kept sacred from the games and the players. Here the nearest relatives are seated, some weeping, or some crooning a lament for the dead, and reciting the virtues of the deceased, but taking no part or interest in the games. Yet much reverence is shown by the people on these occasions. On first entering the cabin,, each person kneels down on the threshold and prays for the repose of the soul of the departed, and several times during the evening, the whole company will kneel down and recite a prayer together, especially when one of the wake tricks is over. Then an old man will rise, take off his hat, and say in a loud voice; "Let us pray for the soul of the dead."

At once the laughter is stilled, and all present join in the prayer with the most grave and solemn demeanor. After this the funeral wail will be raised by the relatives round the corpse, and when it is over, there is a solemn silence for some minutes, which has a most impressive effect. After this the games go on again with renewed vigor, and the laughter and fun is kept up through the night. Then the party breaks up, the young men seeing the girls home, while the mourners are left alone with the dead. These are the customs of a true country wake; but in towns the fun often degenerates into license and drinking, and many games have been therefore forbidden by the priesthood, particularly the one called 'The Mock Marriage,' which often gave occasion to much scandal, and tumult, and fighting among the young men, whereas, in the country wake, it would be deemed a disgrace for a man to create a disturbance, or even lose his temper, and the women and young girls were treated with the utmost respect. No persons of doubtful character were admitted, and the women knew they were safe and protected. The fathers of the village considered it their duty to send their sons to do honor to a dead neighbor, and the mothers sent their girls without fear to the house of death, where they took their places with quiet decorum and joined in the prayers, though quite ready afterwards for the fun, and the laughter, and the curious dramatic games that had been preserved traditionally among the people from the most ancient times.

There is always a plate full of tobacco and another of snuff placed on a table by the side of the corpse, and each man, as he enters, is expected to fill his pipe, and pray in silence for a few moments. While the married people and elders are present, the wake is very solemn; there are no games, but ancient poems are often recited in Irish by the professional story-teller. Then, when the elders leave, about ten o'clock, the fun begins, and all sorts of tricks and jokes are practiced. But at one country wake held not very long ago, and still well remembered by the people, there was no sign of merriment. A beautiful young girl was one day struck dead by lightning while walking in the hayfield with her two young sisters, who were untouched. The children ran home to tell the sad tale, and the greatest consternation prevailed through the country. At the crowded wake held afterwards in her honor, not a laugh was heard, not a trick was played. There was nothing save prayer and weeping, or the deep silence of sorrow, after which the wail of the women would rise up again to almost a shriek of despair. And so passed the whole long night of gloom in tears and lamentations, and bitter cries of the mourning kindred over the fair young form of the dead.

Wake ceremonies are still held in the Irish cabins, where the men drink and smoke, and tell ancient stories, though the highly dramatic games of former times have almost entirely died out; "for," as the peasant narrator added, when concluding his account of the scenes he had witnessed in his early youth, "there is no mirth or laughter to be heard any more in the country; the spirit has gone from our people, and all the old fun is frozen, and the music is dumb in poor Ireland now."

PEASANT TALES

A Night with the Fairies

In a remote part of the mountain district of the West of

Ireland, there dwelt, once on a time, a young man named Denis Ryan, as fine a young fellow as ever lived, and as brave as he was handsome. But his home was very lonely and desolate, for hardly a human being ever came that way. So by degrees he grew weary of his life altogether, and longed to follow the clouds that went sailing away over his head on to the great, wide sea, beyond which were bright, beautiful new lands, where, perhaps, he might be happy. And, finally, he could bear the desolate loneliness no longer, but one day threw up his work and resolved to go down amid the people of the plains, and see if they knew anything of joy and laughter, and the free life that stirs the soul of youth.

So early one morning, before sunrise, he began boldly to descend the mountain, not knowing which path to take, but walked on and on, till he was dead tired, without meeting a soul; when, just at nightfall, as the black darkness was coming on, he came to a rude hut in a lonely glen with nothing but bare heath all around. And the hut looked dreary and queer, but he was so pressed by hunger and fatigue, that he resolved to brave the worst, and, lifting the latch, he entered. No one was there but an old woman crouching over the fire, and she looked very angry, and told him to begone, for that was no place for him to find shelter and food.

"But, mother," he said, "let me rest, for there is no other place in all the country round for miles and miles, and I am weary and hungry after crossing the mountains and traveling since dawn. Let me rest in peace." Then the old woman grew softer and gentler, and let him sit down by the fire, and gave him food. But when he was rested, she told him that he had now better leave at once, as strange people were coming who would be wroth if they saw him, and certainly do him some injury. "Yet, mother," he said, "let me stay till daylight, for I am so weary and in need of rest. Let me stay, in the name of God, and the blessing of the Lord will be on you."

"Hush!" she cried, with an angry voice, "that name is never to be named here. There are people coming who would kill you if you uttered that word before them. Now, mind what I tell you. At midnight they will be here, and you must hold your peace, and be civil and quiet; but ask no questions, and eat no food they may offer you, and beware of making the sign of the Cross, or of naming the Name."

So he watched and waited, and at midnight a tramping was heard outside, as of the rushing of many feet, and the door flew open, and in came a crowd of little men, each wearing a red doublet and cape, and a small cocked hat on the head, with a white feather. They stared at the stranger with bold, fearless eyes, but were not unfriendly; and when the old woman spread out the table with food, they all sat down to supper in the highest glee, and asked the young man to join them and eat. This, however, he refused, saying he had already eaten his supper, thanks to the good, kind lady of the hut; so they let him alone, and were very merry among themselves. And after the food, each man produced a bottle, and drink was poured out in tiny cups with much laughter and merriment. Now when the young wayfarer saw the beautiful red wine, he longed for it so much, that when they offered him a cup he was loth to refuse, but drank it off, and then another and another, though the old woman held up her finger, and made signs to him to warn him of the danger. And after they had all drank, and laughed, and made merry, the chief of the little men rose up and said: "Comrades, it is time we were off, the moon is up, the wine is out, and we must go and search for more. I know of a grand gentleman in the far North who has the best cellars in the whole country round; let us go at once to him, before the day dawns, and while all the household sleep we can fill our bottles and be away before their morning dreams are over." And turning to the stranger, he asked: "Young man, will you go with us?", "Ay, that I will," replied the young fellow, for the wine had made him valiant. "Then here's to the North!" shouted all the little men, and he shouted: "Here's to the North!" as loudly as any of them.

"Then let us be off," said the leader; "but first give our friend here a red cape and a hat with a white feather." So they dressed him up just like one of themselves, and then they all rushed out into the night like a whirlwind of fallen leaves; and presently they stopped before the gate of a stately castle, and the leader just touched the lock and it opened at once; and they entered a great hall and passed down a flight of stairs till they came to a cellar underground, locked and bolted; but the leader just touched the door with his thumb, and it opened freely; and they all went in and filled their bottles, and drank besides, as much wine as they liked of the best and rarest. "Come, now," said the leader at last, "we have had enough. Let us be off to Connaught. This is right good Spanish wine, and we'll know where to find it again; but now we must go before the day dawns."

So they all scampered off again like a rush of leaves before the wind. But Denis had taken so much wine that he was unable to follow them, and he lay helpless on the floor of the cellar. So when morning came, the master of the place coming in found him there fast asleep. "Ah, my fine fellow!" he exclaimed, "have I caught you at last? And all my good Spanish wine spilled about,. and ever so many bottles stolen. You shall hang for this, as sure as fate." So the poor youth was carried off to gaol, and being fairly tried by judge and jury, was condemned to be hanged, for he had no defense to offer. It was quite evident that he had broken open the cellar door and stolen the wine, and consequently deserved his fate.

And when the fatal day came, all the town was crowded

to see young Denis dance the rope-dance; and the priest walked by him saying the prayers, and the hangman stood there holding the cap to cover the face of the poor young man for his execution; and the sheriff looked on to see that all was right and proper. "Now," said the unhappy criminal, speaking up for the last time, "I have just one favor to ask of these good gentlemen before I die. Do not put that ugly thing over my face which the hangman is holding in his hand, but give me my own red cap with the white feather that I had on when I was arrested in the cellar, and let me die with it on my head, and nothing else." Now, the sheriff was a tender-hearted man, and he pitied the young fellow, so he said, "Let him have the cap; go, fetch it for him, and let him die in peace.", "Ay," said Denis, "I shall now die happy," and he took the cap with the white feather in his hand, and placing it at once upon his head, he cried out in a loud voice, "Here's for home!" And then arose a great commotion among all the officials round the gallows, and the sheriff and the priest and the hangman stared at each other speechless with amazement, for the young man had disappeared, cap and all, and from that hour to this no tale or tidings of him could be heard; and the sheriff and the hangman looked very foolish as they made their way home amid the hooting and the laughter of the crowd, who shouted for joy that the gallows had been cheated, for that time at least, of so fine a young fellow for a victim as Denis Kyan.

A LEGEND OF SHARK

On Shark Island there lived some years ago a woman named Mary Callan, with her one only child. Indeed, she never had another, from the fright she got some weeks after her baby was born, and this was her strange story. Suddenly, at dead of night, she was awoke by the child crying, and starting up, she lit the candle, when to her horror she saw two strange men standing beside her bed, and they threw a mantle over her and drew her out of the house into the dark night; and there at the door she saw a horse waiting, and one of them lifted her up, and then sprang up himself, and they rode away like the wind into the darkness.

Presently they came to a great, black-looking house, where a woman was waiting, who brought her in, and she found herself all at once in a splendid hall lit up with torches and hung with silk. And the woman told her to sit down and wait till she was called, as there was very important business for her to attend to. Now, when the woman left her alone, Mary began to look about her with great curiosity, and a large silver pot on the table, filled with sweet-smelling ointment, especially attracted her, so that she could not help rubbing some on her hands, and touched her eyes with the fragrant salve.

Then suddenly a strange thing happened, for the room seemed filled with children, but she knew that they were all dead, for some of them were from her own village, and she remembered their names, and when they died. And as she watched them, one of the children came over quite close, and looking fixedly at her, asked: "What brought you here, Mary, to this dreadful place? For no one can leave it until the Judgment Day, and we dwell for ever in sorrow for the life that has been taken from us. And the men went for your child tonight, to bring it here among the dead, but when you struck a light they could do no harm; yet they are still watching for it, so hasten back, or it will be too late, and the child will die. And tell my mother that I am with the spirits of the hill, and not to fret, for we shall meet again on the Judgment Day."

"But how can I go out in the darkness?" asked Mary, "for I know not my way.", "Never mind," said the child; "here, take this leaf, and crush it close in your hand, and it will guide you safe from harm." And she placed a green leaf in the woman's hand, and on the instant Mary found herself outside the door of the great house, but a tremor fell on. her, for loud voices were heard calling her back, and footsteps seemed to pursue her as she fled away. Then, just as she was sinking to the earth with fright, she grasped the leaf close in her hand, and in a moment she was at her own door, and the footsteps of the pursuers ceased; but she heard a groat cry within the house, and a woman rushed out and seized her arm.

"Come, Mary," she said, "come quickly. Your child is dying. Something is strangling it, and we cannot help or save him."

Then Mary, wild with fear, sprang to the little bed where lay the child, and he was quite black in the face, as if some one was holding him by the throat, but, quick as thought, Mary took the leaf and crushed it into the child's hand. And gradually the convulsion passed away, and the natural color came back, and in a little while he slept peacefully in his mother's arms, and she laid him in his bed and watched by him all night; but no harm came, and no evil thing touched him. And in the morning he smiled up at his mother, bright and rosy as ever, and then she knew that the fairy power was broken, and the child was saved by the spell of the leaf that had come to her from the hands of the dead that dwell in the Spirit Land, And Mary made a case for the leaf, and worked it richly, and tied it round her neck to wear forevermore. And from that day the fairies ceased to molest her, and her child grew and prospered, for the spirits of the dead watched over him to keep him safe from harm.

The Doctor's Visit

The fairies have always an earnest desire for the aid of a mortal physician in sickness, especially if a fairy baby is expected. One evening, late in summer, a servant in rich livery rode up to the house of the chief doctor of Roscommon, and handed him a letter requesting his attendance immediately for a lady of rank, who had been taken suddenly ill, and was in great danger. The doctor, with that alacrity in cases of emergency for which his honorable profession is distinguished, instantly ordered his horse; but as he was quite unacquainted with the locality mentioned, and had never even heard the name of the residence before, he requested the servant to accompany him, and they rode off together at a brisk pace. After a couple of hours' ride they came to a fine house in a park thickly wooded, and there on the steps of the mansion was a grand, stately gentleman awaiting them, like a nobleman in dress and bearing, who received the doctor with great courtesy, and led him into the house, where a number of servants in splendid livery were in attendance.

Having passed through a spacious hall, the doctor and the gentleman entered a gorgeous saloon hung with silk and tapestry, and from that they passed into the lady's sleeping-chamber, when the master of the house withdrew, leaving the doctor alone with the lady, who lay on a gilded couch, with rich silken curtains falling all round her. The doctor lost no time in making use of his professional skill, and with the best results, but all the time the lady had a black veil over her face, and spoke no word. However, when all had ended satisfactorily, the doctor rang the bell, and the gentleman appeared. He made no remark to the veiled lady, but courteously thanking the doctor, handed him forty golden guineas as his fee, and then requested him to come to supper, which was awaiting them in the grand saloon.

There the doctor found many noble guests assembled, and ladies glittering with jewels, and a gorgeous feast covered the table; but he was tired, and threw himself on the sofa to rest, when all the company gathered round him and entreated him to eat and drink. And the master handed him a silver cup of ruby wine, and told him he must drink the lady's health, and he pressed the cup into his hand.

So the doctor was too polite to refuse, and he rose up with the cup in his hand to quaff the wine in honor of the lady, when a beautiful young girl near him touched his foot, and whispered, gently; "Beware of the wine, touch nothing here, it is fatal," and she drew him down again on the sofa, and sat beside him, holding his hand. And it seemed to him nothing on earth could surpass her in beauty, with her golden hair, and glittering eyes; and still she held his hand, and murmured soft words in his ear till a faintness came over him, and gradually his eyes closed in a deep sleep, and he knew nothing more till the sound of his own name, called in a loud voice, aroused him. He started up and looked round. The morning sun was bright in the east, but all the glory and the beauty of the festival had vanished, and he was in a churchyard alone. No, not quite alone, for his faithful servant Terry was beside him, assisting him to rise.

"Where am I?" exclaimed the bewildered doctor, "and what has brought me here?"

"Look there," said Terry, "your honor is just lying on Father Byrne's tombstone. And lucky it is the sign of the Cross is upon it, so I knew your honor was safe when I called you; and glad I am, for I have been looking for you since daylight, and never would have thought of trying the churchyard, only the mare, poor beast, was at the gate, as if trying to get in. Though how your honor came here is a wonder, unless you were carried over the wall, for the gate was locked, and I ran myself to get the key. And it's a hard bed you've had, and a cold bolster," added Terry, rolling away a big stone that bad been placed under the doctor's head for a pillow. "God protect us, master dear, but the good people must have had a hand in this work, and bad luck would have come of it, only your honor lay down on the sign of the blessed Cross, and so your honor is safe this time, anyway."

"Well, Terry, help me up," said the doctor, who was rather benumbed, and a little crestfallen, thinking of that beautiful young creature who had played him such a trick- "and, Terry, go and fetch the mare, for I must be home at once."

So while the mare was coming round, the doctor put his hand in his pocket just to comfort himself with a sight of the golden guineas; but, lo! Nothing was there save a handful of moss, and the doctor rode home a sadder and a wiser man.

Fairy Help

Every district in Ireland has its peculiar and separate fairy chief or king. Finvarra, as every one knows, has his palace on the hill of Knockma, at Tuam, deep under the ground, where the walls are of crystal, and the floor is paved with gold. And he has power over all the fairies of that region, and is adored by them, for he is handsome and splendid, and all the fairy ladies of his Court are beautiful as a garden of roses. But another chief rules over the western sea-coast of the Atlantic, whose name is Fiachra.

Now there was a gentleman of ancient lineage living in that part of the country, of the great race of the O'Haras; and Lochlin O'Hara was noted above all others for the open house and the liberal hand, for he spent his money like a king right royally; but bad times came, he got engaged in a lawsuit which carried off all his money, and Lochlin O'Hara was on the verge of despair, when at last the good news came that the cause was given in his favor, and all the land of his forefathers was to be restored to him. So he resolved to make a great feast to all comers to celebrate his triumph; but when he began to reckon up the numerous friends and relations who were sure to assemble to drink his health, and all the guests from the country round, he grew alarmed, for there was not wine enough in the cellars for them all; and the weather was bad, and no boat could get to Galway. So he thought of Fiachra, the fairy chief, who was always good to the old families, especially the O'Haras; and he wrote him a letter telling of his great need, and asking for the royal help of the fairy king. And he threw the. letter into the sea and waited the result.

Not long, however, had he to wait, for the next day there was a storm along the coast, and a great keg of Spanish wine was flung up on the beach as if from a shipwreck. But O'Hara knew that Fiachra had sent it, and he and his friends feasted and drank right merrily, and in no man's memory had such wine ever been poured out at a feast as Lochlin O'Hara gave on that night to the assembled guests in the home of his fathers. For Fiachra honored the old race because they had ever been good to the fairies, and never meddled with their hunting-grounds, but always respected their raths and mounds, and the ancient hawthorns where they sheltered and lived happily, and danced all night in the moonlight to the fairy music.

The Western Isles

The islanders in these remote places are firm believers in witchcraft to this day, and still practice many strange spells among themselves. There was a man called Ned Flaherty, who was specially suspected by his neighbors as being in league with the Evil One, for, though he had only a small patch of ground, yet he had always plenty of corn to bring to the market, and was rich and well off and wanted for nothing. So they all determined to watch by turns; and one morning the neighbor who was set to spy over the field saw something black going to and fro, each time carrying a grain of corn, which, then it set on the ground and returned for more, till many grains were thus carried away and planted. Then at last the man got near, and saw that it was a hideous black insect doing all the work, and he stooped down and caught it, and put it in a horn snuff-box that he happened to have with him, and shut down the lid close and carried it home.

Now in a little while there was a great commotion, for Flaherty's wife had disappeared, and all the next day they searched for her, but without success. Then the man happening to tell the story of the insect in his snuff-box to a neighbor, "How do you know," said his friend, "but this may be Flaherty's wife you have in the box?"

And Flaherty himself, hearing of the tale, came to the house and heard the whole story, after which he begged the man to come home with him, and bring the box with him and open it in his presence. This the man did, before Flaherty and several of the neighbors, that all might judge of the truth of the strange story. And when the box was opened, out crawled a large black insect like a beetle, and ran direct into the woman's room as hard as it could go. And after a little while out came Mrs. Flaherty, looking very pale, and with one of her fingers bleeding. "What means this blood?" asked the man. "Why," said Flaherty, "when you shut down the box, you snapped off a little bit of the beetle's claw that was outside, so my wife suffers."

Then all the people saw that there was witchcraft in the house, and the Flaherfcys were shunned by every one, and finally they sailed away from the island and were seen no more.

In Shark Island they tell a story of a man called Dermot, whose wife died of a fever, leaving two children, a boy and a girl. The girl died a year and a day after the mother, but the boy thrived well, until one day when the fever seized him, and he cried out that his mother had come for him, and was calling him. And he asked for a drink of water, but there was none in the house. So a girl took a can and ran down to the well to fill it; and as she was stooping down a black shadow fell on her and covered her. Then she saw the dead mother close beside her, and nearly fainted with fright.

"Never fear, Mary alanna," said the woman, "but do as I bid you. When you go home, you will see a black cock by the head of the child's bed. This is the Spirit of Death come to carry away the boy; but you must prevent him. Therefore do as I tell you. Batch a crowing hen and kill her, and sprinkle the blood over the bed, and take ten straws and throw the tenth away, and stir the blood with the rest ; then lay them on the child, and he will sleep and do well." On this the dead woman vanished, and the girl went home and did as she was ordered; the hen was killed, and the blood sprinkled. And the boy slept after the blood touched him, and slept on and on till the morning. Then he sat up and asked for food, and said he was now quite well, and must go and play. So they let him get up, and he was as strong as ever, and no harm came to him any more. And the heart of the father was glad that the child was given back to him through the sprinkling of the blood.

Now it happened that about three months after, a child of one of the neighbors grew sick, and was like to die. Then the man's wife rose up and said; "See, now, our child is like to die, but look how Dermot cured his son through the sprinkling of blood. Let us do the like." So they caught a crowing hen and killed her, and sprinkled the blood over the sick child. But, lo! a terrible thing happened, for the door was flung open,, and in walked two monstrous black cats. "How dare you kill my kitten?" said one of them- "my darling only kitten! But you shall suffer for it.", "Ay," said the other, "we'll teach you how to insult a royal cat again, and kill one of our great race just to save your own wretched child," and they flew at the man and tore his face and hands.

Then the wife rushed at them with the churn-dash,

while the man strove to defend himself with a spade. But all the same the cats had the best of it, and clawed and tore and scratched till the miserable pair could not see for the blood streaming down their faces. Luckily, however, the neighbors, hearing the scrimmage, rushed in and helped to fight the cats; but soon they had to fly, for the cats were too strong for them, and not a soul could stand before them. However, at last the cats grew tired, and after licking their paws and washing their faces, they moved towards the door to go away, first saying to the man; "Now we have done enough to punish you for this time, and your baby will live, for Death can take but one this night, and he has taken our child. So yours is safe, and this we swear by the blood, and by the power of the great king of the cats." So they whisked out of the house, and were never more seen by man or mortal on the island of Shark.

But many other strange things have also happened on the island according to the narration of the islanders, who are extremely accurate in all the details they give, and never exaggerate, only tell the simple truth, which we are bound to accept unquestioned; for the people are too simple to invent. They only tell in their plain, unvarnished idiom, what they have seen or heard. A man and his wife on the island had two children, lovely as angels, and were very happy. But in process of time a third child was born, a son, and he was two inches longer than any baby that ever yet was seen, and had a great head of black hair, and even something like a beard. And he went on growing up fast to three years old, and was as wise as a man, besides eating a power of food.

But after that he dwindled down, and became quite weeshee and no size at all, though he ate as much as ever. And he was queer in his ways, and with his wizened little face looked just like the sprite of an old man or an ugly dwarf. Well, one Sunday the parents went to mass, leaving a young girl to take care of the children. And, while she was out in the garden picking flowers, suddenly she heard the merriest, jolliest dance-tune from the bagpipes, played by some one in the house. That must be Tom the Piper, she said, as she went in; but lo and behold, there was the little imp stuck up in his grandmother's arm-chair, and he playing away with all his might the sweetest music on a set of paper pipes, and with his wizened face looking fifty years old at least. "Oh, the Lord between us and harm!" exclaimed the girl, rushing out of the house, and screaming at the top of her voice: "Help! help! sure it's the devil himself is sitting there, and not the child at all!"

And the neighbors ran when they heard the screams, and went back with her into the house, but not a sign of the little imp was to be seen, though, after much searching he was discovered behind the meal-tub, a mere little sheeoge, not the size of a sod of turf, and burned black as any coal, and quite dead, stiff and stark, with the withered face of an old, old man. So they all knew he was a witch-child. And when the parents came home they had him put outside on the shovel, and before night he was gone; the devil or the fairies had carried him away. And right glad were the man and his wife to be so well rid of the imp of Satan, who was never more seen or heard of in the house from that hour.

The islanders seem to live for ever in the presence of the spiritual; and every event of their lives, whether for good or ill luck, is attributed to the influence of unseen beings, who are sometimes good, but more often malign to mortals. Every sickness or accident or misfortune is believed to be the work of the invisible Sidhe, or fairy race; and all the primitive science of the people, their knowledge of herbs, and of powerful charms and incantation, is used to break the spells and counteract the sinister designs of the active sprites who haunt the house, and are especially anxious to get possession of the children and carry them off to the fairy homes. A pretty little girl was out one day weeding in the turnip-field, when a sudden blast swept over the place, and gave her a chill, so that she lost the use of her limbs for the time, and was carried home and put to bed. Six months she lay there, and grew thinner and thinner, till she looked like a little old woman. So the people saw at last that she was fairy-struck, and no doubt was away every night with the fairies on the hill, though she seemed to be lying there helpless in her bed. And they beat her and starved her to make her tell them how she got away, and what she did when with the fairies.

But the poor child cried to them, "Sure, I am little Mary, and never a foot have I stirred out since you laid me in this bed." Yet not a word would they believe, and set to work to make a powerful fairy potion of known potency against witch-work; three drops to be poured into her ear and three drops down her throat, and the remainder to be used for washing her. And they sent for a wise fairy-woman to see what could be done. But Mary said, "I will not drink the potion. Let me die, for then I shall go to heaven and be at peace."

"Well," said the wise woman, "there is one thing yet may be done to break the devil's spell that is over the child, and if that fails she must die. Let her father carry her to the bog every morning before sunrise, and dip her down for twice seven days in the name of the Holy Trinity and the blessed saints. And if that does not help and cure her, then the power of the Evil One is too strong, and I can do no more. But let her father try it, in the name of God."

So each morning for twice seven days the father carried the child to the bog, and dipped her down before the sun had risen. And gradually her health and strength returned, and at the end of the twice seven days, on the final day of the cure, she was able to walk all the way back to her own place. And the weakness passed from her limbs, and the color and beauty came back to her face, for the spell of the fairies was broken at last through the words of the wise woman, and her power over the spirits of evil.

PEASANT TALES OF THE DEAD

The Specter Bride

In one of the southern villages there was once a beautiful young girl who promised her lover, by the sign of the blessed Cross, that she would marry no one else save him alone. But her parents objected, and forbid him the house, and told her she must never more see him, or walk with him, or talk with him; for they wanted her to marry a rich old farmer, a widower, who lived near by. Then the poor girl fell into a black despair, and determined to kill herself. So, in the madness of her sorrow, she came to the rock of St. Finian to fulfill her intention, and cast herself down from thence into the river and was drowned.

Now it happened that the next night the young man she so dearly loved came by that way, and she appeared to him suddenly. And when he beheld her, he was so enchanted that he tried to throw his arms around her, for he had no fear; but she waved him back, and told him he must not touch her, or put a hand on her, else she would have to go back to the dead, and he would see her no more. But he might take hold of the corner of her apron, and walk with her in the moonlight for a little while. So they wandered by the river's bank until the hour came when the dead must go back to the dead, and she faded away in the moonlight, telling him that she would meet him again at the same spot the following night.

And so he met her a second time, and they walked as before till the midnight hour; but on the third night she told him to come no more, as she meant to go and visit him at his own place, where he lived, though he must tell no one, nor allow any one to see her; therefore, she would not come till dead of night, when he would be all alone.

Now the next night, when the hour was near for the meeting, he grew terribly frightened, and could not help telling a friend and asking his advice. "This do," said the friend. "Take a large, black-handled knife from the farmyard, and place it between yourself and her whenever and wherever she appears; for as long as the knife is there between you she can do you no harm- of this be certain."

So he got the knife as desired, and laid it down across the door of the barn where he slept, and. went and lay down, thinking he was safe. And exactly at midnight she came, and tried to enter through the door, but could not, and he heard the sorrowing wail of her voice outside. But there was a chink in the wall at the opposite side of the barn, quite close to his bed, and through this he heard her trying to force her way, so he made a dash for the knife, and laid it in his bed just as she glided in through the split in the wall. Then she talked long to him, and told him how she loved him, and asked as a favor if he would only let her lie down at his feet on the bed till the hour came when they must part; but as she lay down, her hand happened to touch the knife that was between them, and she fell back with a fearful cry. "Now," she said, "the power I had over you is gone, and the spell is broken that gave me life for a moment; for by means of that knife which you have placed between us, we are parted for ever. Alas! we might have had a happy bridal, but now I must go back to the dead for evermore." and so saying, she laid her hand upon his face, and left him blind all the days of his life; and then the pale ghost of the girl rose up from the bed, and disappeared in a flash of fire, leaving the unhappy lover senseless from terror.

The Witch-Girl

A long while ago there was a young lad employed about the Castle at Castle Derby, and he had a deal of work to do from morning to night, find was often weary of his life by reason of the work. So one evening, when the sunset was on the hills, he threw himself down on the grass to rest, and as he lay there, half in a dream, he was aware of some one bending over him, and on looking up, he beheld a young girl with long golden hair, draped all in white, standing in the red glow of the sunset, and her eyes, like glittering stars, were fixed upon him with a love-light in them that made him tremble. At once young Dermot sprang to his feet, and taking her two hands in his, questioned her as to where she had come from, and why she was watching him while he slept. "Because I love you," she answered, "and pity you, and I have come to help you in the work."

So she stayed till the dark of the evening came on, and helped him to herd the cattle and set the farmyard in order, for she was fleet of foot and firm of hand, and the beasts and fowl followed quietly wherever she led. And the next day she came also, and the next, and worked so well that Dermot had scarcely anything to do at last, except to look at her beautiful eyes, and listen to her sweet singing, as he lay on the grass when the work was all over. At length, however, a sad time came for the lovers, for one day she told him that perhaps he would see her no more, as her people had sent for her. And he was sorely grieved, and fell down on the earth weeping. Then she comforted him, and promised if all ended well that she would see him soon again, and go on with their work and happy life together. But now she must leave; for her kindred were summoned to a battle far away, and it was her place to watch by the wounded. Yet she also might be slain; who could say if her life would be given to her? So let him heed the sign she gave him by which he would know if she were living. And the sign she gave him was this: "Go" she said, "tomorrow evening at sunset to the well near this, where we have so often been together, and if you see the water red, like blood, then you may know that I am dead, and you will never, never see me more. So take this ointment, and in the morning rub it into your eyes, and if I am dead you will see my funeral passing this way, where we have been so happy." And she laid a little box of ointment in his hand, and disappeared.

Now the next day Dermot waited very impatiently till evening to visit the well; but, when he saw the water in the sunset light, lo, it was red like blood; and his bitter cries rose up, and lamentations, so that no one could comfort him, nor could he tell to any one the story of his lost love, for she had bound him to silence. He couldonly cry aloud "My friend, my friend is dead. I shall see her no more."

Now the next day, when the funeral was to pass, he rubbed the ointment on his eyes, and presently he saw it coming along the road, but the sight of the coffin made him quite frantic, and he clapped his hands and tore his hair, like one in madness. Then the men who bore the coffin, seeing his state, stopped in pity, and asked him would he like to see the face of the girl once more, for they were touched by his prayers and tears, and they opened the lid; but when he looked into the coffin, in place of the beautiful girl he had loved, there lay in her shroud the form of a hideous old hag, with long, protruding teeth, that came down over her lips and reached to her chin like the fangs of a wild beast, and as he screamed in horror she lifted one skinny hand and tried to clutch him, while her eyes rolled as if they would start from her head; but he fled away, and never again did the witch-girl appear to him living or dead. And a sadness was on him all his life long for ever after.

The Headless Horses

All the world one time was going to the great fair at Navan, and among them was one Denis Molony, a cow-jobber, a well-to-do, honest man, who had cattle along with him to sell at the fair. But when he reached the outside of the town, night was coming on black dark; so he thought he'd wait awhile, and just let the cattle graze as they liked, while he laid himself down under the hedge till the morning. At that moment, however, a loud moaning and screaming came to his ear, and a woman rushed past him all in white, as if a winding-sheet were round her, and her cries of despair were terrible to hear. Then, after her, a great black coach came thundering along the road, drawn by two black horses; but when Denis looked close at them, he saw that the horses had no heads, and the coachman had no head, and out sprang two men from the coach, and they had no heads either; and they seized the woman, and carried her by force into the carriage, and then drove off.

Now Denis was terribly frightened, and he went back on the road to a house he had passed some time before, and narrated all he had seen to the people, on which they told him that the woman he saw was an evil lover, and a wicked sinner, and no doubt the devils were carrying her off from the churchyard, for she had been buried that morning. But never a prayer would she say, nor make confession to the priest before her death, so God and the holy saints had given her up to punishment, and the devil had his own at last. But to make sure, they went next morning to the churchyard to examine the grave, and there sure enough was the coffin, but it was open, and not a trace of the dead woman was to be seen. So they knew that an evil fate had come on her, and that her soul was gone to eternal torture.

The Woman with the Teeth

The road to Navan has always had an unlucky reputation, and formerly it was considered very dangerous to persons traveling alone between dark and midnight; for it was haunted by a ghost, who appeared sometimes as a bag or a pack of wool rolling along, and no hands touching it, or as a shrouded woman with gleaming white teeth, or sometimes as a dog, the worst of all shapes for a ghost to appear in. And many persons were killed by this ghost, and were found in the morning lying dead, with a black mark round the throat, as if they had been strangled. So great fear was on the people, and few dared to venture on the road after dark. But there was a fine young farmer one time at the fair at Navan, and after drinking and making merry with his friends, he declared that he would go home by that road and no other, and he would fight the ghost, and not leave a shred of it together.

So he mounted his horse and rode off just as night was falling; and all seemed clear on the road for some distance as he went on, when suddenly a woman sprang across the path, and leaped up behind him on the horse before he could hinder her. And she put her two arms round his waist and bade him look round at her beautiful white teeth, for there were no such teeth in all the country round. But he would not. Then she tried to entice him many times to look at her; for it was by this means she killed her victims, the moment they looked at her their doom was certain. The young man, however, had a brave, resolute heart, and he told her he would not look at her then, but he would bring her home with him, and as they sat by the fire in his own house he might take a look at her wonderful teeth, and be the best of good company to her and treat her well. With that he took off his broad leather belt and slung it round her, buckling it again fast to his own body, so that she could not move; and then the two rode home as quick as the wind, and never a word more did she speak. Now when he reached his house, all the people were waiting outside to see what had become of him, and they set up a great shout of laughter when he rode up; for there, buckled round his waist at the back, was a great log of wood, but no sign of the woman. So he unstrapped the wood, and afterwards chopped it up into small pieces, and from every piece fell drops of blood. And then they all saw that it was devil's work; so he flung the pieces outside; but next morning when he went to look for the wood it was all gone. And from that time forth the evil ghost disappeared, to the great comfort of the people. Thus the young farmer did a good piece of work by that night's ride.

The Punishment

There was once upon a time a man of very evil repute, named Donegan, who lived all alone by himself in a wretched little hut close by the bog of Allen. And no one knew how he got any money at all to live by, unless it was by robbery and murder; for he did no work, and neither tilled nor planted. So all the people were afraid of him, and said he was a tool of the devil. And no one would venture near his hut, or have any dealings with him, or say, "God save you kindly" when they met him on the road. But he cared nothing, only looked at them askance from under his shaggy brows, and went on his way in silence. For he himself liked to be alone, and would never let any one, not even the priest himself, cross his threshold.

Now there was no window in the hut, only an open slit to let in the daylight, and when night came he used to put a good wisp of straw and a plank of wood over the opening to keep all safe. But one night, after he was in bed, he heard the sound of some one trying to push away the plank, as if to enter the hut. Now, Donegan knew that no one would come in to rob, for there was nothing to steal, and he also knew that none of the neighbors or villagers would venture to his hut at such a time of night, though someone might come just to annoy him, he was so hated by the people; so he sprang up, and pressed against the plank to keep it from moving. But all was of no use; the force outside was too strong, and in a moment Donegan was flung flat on the floor on his back, and the plank along with him, and a great, tall, strange man entered and stood beside him, wearing a mask over his face. Now, Donegan was strong and fierce, and accustomed to fight for his life, and leaping to his feet at once, he hit the stranger a terrible blow, full in the face; but to his surprise, the blow went right through him, as if he were but air, and left no mark. Still Donegan was not to be frightened.

"Man or devil," he shouted, "you shall not escape me," and he hit him another tremendous blow. Yet he was only beating the air, and the man never moved, but stood fixed, staring with red, fiery eyes through his mask. Then Donegan grew furious. "I never was afraid yet," he cried, "of father or mother, priest or parson, God or hell, and I am not afraid of you, even if you are a ghost from the dead." And he tried to hurl the man to the ground, but still he only struck the air.

Then, at last, the ghost lifted up his arm and took the mask from his face, and Donegan saw before him the terrible, ghastly features of the murdered dead, come from the grave to take vengeance on the murderer, and he fell to the ground helpless and paralyzed with fear; but the ghost had no mercy, he clutched the unhappy wretch, and dashed him against the wall of the hut, then followed and clutched him again and dashed him back to the opposite wall, and so continued till Donegan was almost senseless. Then the ghost left him, for the hour had come when the dead return to their graves; but before his departure he clasped Donegan round the wrist and burned a red circle right through to the bone, saying: "Now you will believe there is a devil, and that the fires of hell are waiting for your sinful soul."

After this fearful adventure, Donegan lost all strength and power, and sent for the priest, to whom he made a full confession of his many crimes, too terrible to be uttered to any other ears; but that same night he disappeared, and no one knew from that day forth whither he had gone, or what became of him. He left no sign, and was never seen afterwards by living man; but the people believe that he was carried off bodily by the devil himself, for an evil fate was on him, and both in life and death he was accursed.

Irish Minstrelsy

Music was held in much repute in the ancient world as a curative agent, besides being the inspiration that gave force to life, stimulating or soothing as the moment required; for music, above all arts, has a subtle power over the nervous system, and is able to interpret and direct all the sudden, swift, and varied phases of human emotion. It can stir the soul to its inmost depths till the tears fall in silent sorrow, or fill the brain with a passionate enthusiasm, which is a prophecy of victory. All the great nations of antiquity recognized the relation between emotion and music. Plato made it a direct educational agent, even as Pythagoras had done when he showed the people how, by its wonderful power, it could melt the soul to divine pity, or kindle it to the sublime madness that creates great deeds.

The Irish, from the earliest times, have shown their belief in the mystic influence of music upon life; and their legends record how the musician could soothe the wounded or calm the dying, and even make those in agony forget their pains. At the festivals and religious ceremonies, and the banquets of kings and chiefs, the bard swept the chords of the harp till the waves of human passion surged or fell in rhythmic harmony with the bardic song. And, above all men, at the royal Court, the bard was honored for his divine gift. He was given a noble income by law, freely and of grace, to lift him above the necessity of servile cares.

His place at the royal table was next the monarch, and above the nobles, and wearing his robe of seven colors, and the circlet of gold upon his brow, he sat a prince among princes. But civilization no longer recognizes the true mission of music as a redemptive power, able to calm the nerves or exorcise the evil spirit, when the soul sinks under the shadow of coming sorrow. Even our hospitals never seem to think of utilizing music as a curative agent, either to lull pain or waken the dormant faculties to a new sense of the joy of life, yet the wards are often filled with the rich perfume of flowers sent by loving hands, though flowery, unlike music, may be at times a dangerous, even a deadly offering to the sick. Music, however, still retains its subtle, spiritual influence over the Irish heart, and no great political movement was ever yet inaugurated in Ireland without the aid of the priesthood of song; but as a powerful agent to relieve pain or act on the nervous system, music is no longer used, as formerly, by the fairy-doctor or the wise woman of the village to help or to effect a cure.

Thus, in the direction of therapeutics, its use seems to have wholly ceased; but, as a spiritual power, it can still excite and inspire the Irish nature with the same vivid force that in old times made music supreme above all other arts in its mystic influence upon the human soul. A recent volume of Irish poems, collected and edited by Mr. Halliday Sparling, ('Irish Minstrelsy,' by Halliday Sparling. London, Canterbury Series.) proves that the instinctive tendency of the Irish people to set their wrongs to music still exists as vividly as ever. Music and song have illustrated all the great epochs of modern Irish history; the era of Grattan and the Volunteers of O'Connell and Emancipation, when Moore, in his 'Lalla Rookh,' under the disguise of 'The Fire Worshipers,' incarnated the fierce resolve of Catholic Ireland to break the bondage of the penal yoke. And then came the era of

1848, when the intellect of the nation received its most splendid impulse, and with the noblest results. Emancipation had been gained, and the Catholics of Ireland, after two centuries of insult and degradation, were just then beginning to feel and know that they had human rights, and strength to gain them if they so willed. But the utterance of a people, though always vehement, is often incoherent, and then it is that the men of education and culture are needed to interpret and formulate the vague longings and ambitions of the passionate hearts around. Thus the literature of 1848, under the guidance of eminent and gifted men, became the glowing incarnation of the desire of a whole people to raise their country to a fitting place among the nations, and the spirit-power was the mighty force they used to overthrow narrow intolerance and prejudice, and to give the fierce, popular instincts for right and justice, a higher direction than mere reckless revenge over the oppressor.

The leaders soon gathered round them by elective affinity all the glowing genius of the country, an impassioned race of poets and orators, famous afterwards in the history of the period as the 'Young Ireland' party, whose words of power, to use Chaucer's phrase, were "like a trumpet thundering" in the ears of the people. The poets, above all, touched the heart of the nation, when, with a madness of inspiration, they chanted the wrongs and hopes of the people in rhythmic words. Most of the songs in Mr. Sparling's collection date from this period, when the whole life of the nation moved to music. Even the peasants and artisans of the time became poets, and some of their strong, fiery verses, the product of powerful emotion, show how even the rudest elements were kindled and transfigured by the glory of the new light.

Thomas Davis, the chief of this young band of thinkers and workers, was an incarnation of passionate genius- the most powerful of the poets, the most brilliant of the essayists. His words, like a fiery cross, flashed through the length and breadth of the land, awakening mind, heart, and brain, from the dull apathy of centuries of oppression. With the tempest in his soul, and the lightning on his lips, he poured out for the people the divine wine of intellect that lifts humanity from the animal to the god. But his brief life of work for Ireland soon ended; it was scarcely more than a three years' fever, and then in the very prime of his youth and genius, and the full triumph of his successful leadership, as with a rainbow gleam he sprang into the sunlight and so died. He is well represented in the selections by several of his most striking poems; 'Fontenoy,' and 'The Geraldines', 'The Volunteers of '82,' and others as celebrated and as popular. Charles Gavan Duffy, however, as editor of The Nation, had the chief direction of the new movement. A man of the highest culture, of exquisite literary taste, and a clear and powerful writer, both in prose and verse, lie was eminently fitted for guide and counselor to all the young, fiery intellects that composed his staff, while his winning manners and earnest sympathy with all that was noble and beautiful in literature and art gained their admiration and love.

As a poet he stands in the first rank of the national bards. One of his best poems, 'The Muster of the North' by the strong, fierce music of the rhythm, shows the true Celtic fire and force of his nature. The leaders of Young Ireland were often likened to the men of the great French Revolution. Gavan Duffy was the Vergniaud, the organizer and inspirer. Meagher, in his beautiful youth, and with the passionate fervor of his eloquence, was the St. Just without his cruelty. John Mitchell, strong in words and powerful in purpose, was Danton, with his fearless gospel of audacity; while Isaac Butt, with his tossed masses of black hair, his flashing eyes, and splendid rush of classic oratory, was the Mirabeau of the party. Smith O'Brien was honored as leader, from his lineage and rank.

Stately as a king, of rare and stainless honor, he seemed never to forget that he was the descendant of kings, and might even one day claim the title himself, if the revolution succeeded. John Dillon, father of the young patriot of the present day, was a grand specimen of the Spanish-Irish type, and the southern fire ran warm through his veins. He was one of the most impassioned speakers of the gifted band, and no assembly could resist the volcanic torrent of his burning words. These were the orators of Young Ireland. Like the Girondists, they set up a lofty ideal for humanity; to regenerate the people by culture, noble aims, noble lives, and the service of solemn devotion to their country. But there was no Marat among them; they had no plans of cruel vengeance and plunder, they counseled no crimes, their lives were as pure as their doctrines, and not a shadow rests upon their fair fame. As a poet described them, so were they:

> "Souls of fire like columns pointing
> Flamelike upward to the skies,
> Glorious brows which God's anointing
> Consecrated altar-wise;
> Stainless hearts, like temples olden
> None but priests hath ever trod,
> Hands as pure as were the golden
> Staves that bore the Ark of God."

Yet these singers and scholars, these brilliant young orators and writers, who showed to what height Irish genius might rise if trained and guided, with their sublime ideal of nationhood and heroic means of action, were deemed more dangerous by England than even the assassin's knife, for enlightenment means independence. But the selections in Mr. Sparling's work are not limited to one party or one theme. Every name of note down to the present day, and all political tendencies, with every chord that has vibrated to Celtic sentiment and feeling, will be found in the collection, making this pretty volume of Irish minstrelsy the most interesting and the most comprehensive compendium of national poetic genius yet given to the public. About twenty names will be found in the list of poets. Among them Florence McCarthy, the translator of Calderon; and Sir Samuel Ferguson, the bard and Brehon, who took the rude legends of early history and transfigured them by his poetic power into the stately majesty of national epics; and John Francis Waller, the sweetest living lyrist of Ireland, who unites all the subtle charm of faultless form and tender grace with perfect melody. And the weird fancies of Clarence Mangan are not forgotten; nor the spiritual delicacy and fine touch of William Allingham, nor the classic verse of Aubrey de Vere, glowing in thought and carefully chiseled, with well-skilled workmanship, contrasting well with the rough-hewn rocks of Banim's powerful verse streaked with rich veins of gold. And we have the playful humor of Sam Lover, that turns to music in the utterance; and the pathetic beauty of Lady Dufferin's songs, like the well known "I'm sitting on the stile, Mary," which has been steeped in the tears of two hemispheres; and the fierce defiance of Ingram's great poem, 'Who fears to speak of '98;' while the strong minstrelsy of the fiery North is illustrated by such ballads as Colonel Blacke's famous 'Still put your trust in God, my boys, but keep your powder dry;' and the stirring strains of 'The Boyne Water' and 'No Surrender;' poems still chanted at all convivial meetings by the strong Ulster men, who always mean what they say and sing. Nor is Dion Boucicault omitted, with his intensely Irish grace, music, fun, and pathos. There are, besides, quite a number of the peasant and street ballads, with all their floating philosophy and picturesque idiom correctly given for the first time in a poetical anthology, such as 'The Wearing of the Green' so dear to the popular heart; the quaint and mystic Shan-van-Vocht, with its mysterious and cryptic meaning, and the rollicking humor of such ballads as 'The night before Larry was stretched' with all its rich vernacular Dublin slang that recalls the almost extinct race of wandering blind Homers, of which the eminent 'Zozimus' was perhaps the last representative. Happily, also, we find in the minstrelsy the last great poem that has attained marked celebrity- 'God save Ireland,' by T. D. Sullivan, M.P., late Lord Mayor of Dublin, the most ardent and powerful of the living Irish poets.

This spirited chant, which has all the strong, musical beat for which Mr. Sullivan's verses are noted, at once took the heart of the people by storm, and the chorus, caught up and echoed by twenty millions of the Irish race, was heard throughout the world:

"God save Ireland! say we proudly,
God save Ireland, say we all,
Whether on the scaffold high,
Or the battlefield we die,
O what matter, when for Erin dear we fall."

All these illustrations of the passionate genius of Ireland find a place in Mr. Sparling's 'Pantheon of Poets.' And he well deserves the thanks of all true lovers of song for the admirable manner in which he has fulfilled his task, and the lucid arrangements of his materials. All the various strings of the Irish harp have been touched, and made to give up the strange, fitful, and wayward music that can move at will to tears or laughter,, and which never fails to vibrate in the Irish heart. For music and song are part of the life of the people; they give a glow to the stormy twilight of their troubled lives, and strength to bear the tragic terrors of a bitter destiny. Through music and song the Irish race has always uttered the strongest emotions of the vivid Celtic nature, and their poets and orators have ever had a sovereign power to lift them above the relentless tortures of privation and persecution, and to redeem them from the darkness of despair.

ANCIENT CURES, CHARMS, AND USAGES OF IRELAND

The passionate dreams of political enthusiasts may pass away, but the literary value of the songs remain as a richly illuminated page of Irish history. Nothing really good in a nation's life is ever lost. It remains an influence for all time, and the people will never now go back to the servile bondage of soul and spirit that held them enchained before the fetters were rent and the bonds broken by the genius and intellectual force, the lofty teaching, and the cadenced words of the men of '48.

Ancient Irish Gold

There is every reason to believe that gold existed abundantly in Ireland in former times, and the mines of the South were worked, and the gold smelted in the various gold districts, probably a thousand years before the Christian Era. The earliest race, however, the men of the Stone Age, do not seem to have had any knowledge of metals, and no gold ornaments have been found in the ancient crannoges, or lacustrine habitations, or with the earliest remains of the dead. But the next race, the Tuatha-de-Danans, were skilled in metallurgy, and eminent as artificers in gold and silver; so that in the popular belief they were held to be necromancers, and in league with the fairies and the spirits of the hill.

Dianecht, the chief smith of the Tuatha-de-Danans, still holds an enduring place in Irish tradition for his skill in the production of an artificial hand, fashioned of silver, which he made for Nuadhe, the king, who had lost his own hand in the great battle fought with the Firbolgs for the possession of Ireland, and in confirmation of this story the king is henceforth known in history as 'Nuadhe of the silver hand.'

The Milesians who followed and conquered the Tuatha, were a Celtic-Spanish race, according to tradition, and from them the chief existing noble families of Ireland claim descent, such as the O'Neills, the O'Connors, the O'Briens, and others, whose descendants are still honoured by the people for their ancient and noble blood. The Milesians were a splendid and powerful people, wise and learned, who, after the conquest of Ireland, became the founders of a just and extended code of laws, and of a well-defined political social system. To this great Milesian race may be attributed the vast quantity of manufactured gold which has been dug up from time to time from the soil and bogs of Ireland.

The ancient bardic legends and poems make frequent mention of the costly personal decorations worn by the kings and queens, the chiefs and princes, bards and Brehons; the massive torques, diadems, amulets, rings, and brooches; the gold trapping for the horses, the rich clasps for the royal mantles, and other ornaments of beautiful form and workmanship, all made by the native goldsmiths, who had a certain fixed size and weight for each ornament to suit the rank of the wearer. Even the very nature of the ornament was specified by law. Thus we read, that by command of one of the chief monarchs of Erin, at all the great festivals held at the Court of Tara, the princes were ordered to wear torques of gold and chains upon the neck, to distinguish them from the common people; and the nobles, rings of gold upon the fingers.

The bards were distinguished by a golden fillet round the brow, while the queens and royal ladies bound their long flowing locks with the circlet, or asion of gold. And we find it related of Maeoe, the great Queen of Connaught, that when going to battle she rode in an open chariot, accompanied by four other chariots before her, behind her, and one on each side, to keep the golden asion on her head, and her royal robes from being defiled by the dust raised by the tramp of the horses and the men-at-arms as they rushed by. For all the sovereigns of Erin sat crowned as they drove in their war-chariots to battle, as well as at the public feasts and ceremonies.

Gold rings were also used as current money for barter, tribute, or reward. And the victor in a battle was often styled 'The Exactor of Rings,' because of the ransom he demanded from the vanquished. Of Queen Boanna, wife of the Poet- King of Munster, who gave her name to the River Boyne, it is told that, when she sat at the festivals beside the king, she had her arms covered with rings of gold, ready for bestowal on the poets who pleased her best by their recitations.

In the ancient 'Book of Rights,' gold-adorned shields are mentioned, also gold trappings for the horses, gold-trimmed cloaks and tunics, and. Rings of 'the red gold.' The amount of gold given on various occasions is also distinctly stated by the chroniclers. Thus, Brian Boru, the king, made an offering of twenty ounces of gold at the shrine of St. Patrick; and Dermot MacMorrough, who first brought the Normans over to Ireland, gave a hundred ounces of gold to O'Rourke, Prince of Bresney, as an einach, or atonement, for having carried off his wife; while Devorgill, the fatal and faithless spouse, when, repentant and sorrowful after seeing the invasion of her country, she entered the Abbey of Melifont to end her days, made an offering on the altar of a golden chalice, along with twenty ounces of gold, as an expiation for her sin.

When the King of Ulster visited Tara, the chief monarch of Ireland was bound to present him with a minn, or lunula, a crescent-shaped ornament for the head, 'of the full breadth of his face in gold.' And the provincial kings had rings of gold upon every finger. Caps of gold were frequently offered by one king to another, and the tribute paid annually to the chief monarch by the minor kings included steeds with golden bridle-bits, and cloaks with golden clasps, swords, shields, and numerous caps of gold. The drinking-horns and wine-cups were inlaid with gold; the sacred shrines were plated with gold, and encrusted with jewels; and the golden chalices, and other adornments for altar service, were of such splendor that the churches were frequently plundered by the Danes and other piratical Norsemen, for the sake of the rich spoil. In 1169, 'The Four Masters' record that Donogh O'Canoll, Lord of Airghialla, gave, when dying, three hundred ounces of gold to the clerics and churches for the love of God. From costly gifts of this kind, made by the kings and nobles, a vast amount of treasure was accumulated in the abbeys and monasteries, much of which became the prey of the rude invaders, and was carried off by them to their northern home.

As no native gold is found in Denmark, it is supposed that the Danes melted down the Irish gold, and then fashioned vessels and ornaments after their own manner, giving them the distinctive impress of Scandinavian art; and thus the presence of so many gold articles in the great northern museums may be accounted for. The amount of ancient manufactured gold which has been found in Ireland is almost incredible. No other country in north-western Europe possesses so much belonging to early times; and it is remarkable that the same special character of ornamentation can be traced throughout all these magnificent specimens, called by Kemble the Opus Hibernicum, proving that they were the genuine product of Irish artistic skill.

In 1802, ten golden bracelets, of the open shape common to Egypt and the Bast, were found in Connaught, buried deep down in a bog, and sold afterwards for seven hundred pounds-the mere value in weight. In 1854, while making the Ennis railway, the workmen came upon a vast number of gold ornaments, all in one hoard. This great 'Clare Find,' as it is called, was discovered deep down in the ground, packed together in a little stone receptacle, the ornaments being neatly piled one upon the other, and covered with clay. The hoard comprised one hundred and thirty-seven rings of gold, numerous torques, gorgets, fibulae, bracelets, circlets, amulets, and other ornaments, all of pure gold, and bright as if just fresh from the goldsmith's hand, the value being estimated at five thousand pounds in mere weight, without considering the perfect workmanship. The hoard was supposed to be the spoil of a foray, carefully secreted by the victors, but never removed, probably from some adverse chance of war; and so the precious deposit had remained hidden and untouched in the earth for more than a thousand years.

A second hoard was discovered some time after when cutting another portion of the railway, of the value of two thousand pounds. Many of these costly articles were secured for the National Museum of the Royal Irish Academy, which now contains above three hundred specimens of manufactured gold, forming the most interesting Celtic collection to be found in Europe. The British Museum also obtained some specimens from the great 'Clare Find,' but a large portion disappeared in the smelting-pot. Gold diadems have been frequently found in the soil or the bogs. There are ten in the Dublin Museum, weighing from four to sixteen ounces. The finest was discovered twelve feet deep in a bog, in the County Limerick, and measures above eleven inches in height. The form is perfect and beautiful, having large gold discs to finish off the ends at the ears, and the ornamentation is, in the highest degree, artistic.

There are also thirty-seven gold torques in the museum, two of them being the most splendid specimens known, measuring above five feet in, length, and each being more than twenty-seven ounces in weight. They were discovered in 1810 by a peasant boy, at Tara, the ancient Court of the Kings, and after many vicissitudes, these costly historic relics found their way into the possession of the late Duke of Sussex, but were finally purchased by the Royal Irish Academy.

The torque, as a personal decoration, was well known to

the ancient world, to Egypt, Persia, and, later, to the Romans. It can be seen in the Pompeian Mosaics and on the neck of 'The Dying Gladiator;' and it is a well-known historic fact that the name Torquatos was given to Titus Manlius and his race for having taken a torque from the neck of a Celtic Gaul in battle. But, above all, it seems to have been the favorite ornament of the Celtic chiefs, and more golden torques have been found in Ireland, and of greater size, than exist in any Continental collection.

The torque (or tore in Irish), was in form a large hoop made of twisted ropes of gold, and was worn on the neck, or round the waist. The size and splendor of these magnificent personal ornaments show the instinctive love of the Irish for bright and glittering decorations. It is recorded of Cormac Mac-Art, who reigned at Tara, that he sat at the banquet crowned with gold, wearing a fine, purple garment, a golden brooch on his breast, a collar or tore of gold round his neck, and a belt adorned with gold and precious stones encircling his waist. In the museum of Trinity College, Dublin, there is a fibula of pure gold, eight and a half inches long, and weighing thirty-five ounces, the heaviest as yet known to exist. It was no doubt one of the ancient regal ornaments used to fasten the mantle of the king on the shoulder.

Of the lunette (called minn or meend in Irish), there are eighteen specimens in the Royal Irish Academy, from five to eleven inches high, and there are three in the British Museum, brought over from Ireland. They were worn by chiefs, and the victors in a battle, and by royal ladies. It is recorded of Maireen, Queen of Dermot, chief monarch at Tara, that being bald, she wore one on her head to cover the defect; but a favorite of King Dermot's, being jealous of her, bribed a woman to tear the golden minn from the queen's head as she sat at the festival surrounded by the princes and nobles. "May God preserve me!"

exclaimed Maireen, when she was conscious of the insult, placing her hand upon her head, when lo! before any of the Court had time to look, or mock at her, a flowing mass of golden hair fell down upon the queen's shoulders, covering her with its beauty. And thus she triumphed over her enemies. Manufactured gold is generally found in Ireland hidden deep in the bogs, or, in isolated specimens of great value, in the vicinity of the ancient forts and battle-grounds, as if dropped by the vanquished in a hasty retreat, or buried, on some sudden surprise, for fear of the plundering invader.

The south-west is richer in these treasures than the north-west; but they are scattered broadcast over the country. The soil of Ireland seems literally strewn with gold, and many rich hoards will, no doubt, be discovered in time, according as the bogs are drained, or new cuttings for railroads made through the remote districts of the South and West. Unfortunately, large quantities have been already destroyed and lost, from the ignorance of the finders respecting the antiquarian value of the articles, or through fear of detection; but chiefly from the absence of all law of treasure-trove, the present law, chiefly obtained through the valuable services and exertions of the late learned and gifted Lord Talbot-de-Malahide, having only come into operation in the year 1861.

Before that period the jewelers purchased largely from the finders for the purpose of melting down the gold. The leading goldsmiths of the present day estimate that within the last few years upwards of ten thousand pounds' worth of gold ornaments have passed into the crucible. A splendid fibula from one of the finds was sold for fifty-two guineas, its exact weight, and so has been lost to the national collection. But now, by the law of treasure-trove, the finder, if he brings the article to the nearest police-station, is given a receipt, with the promise of full value to be paid by the Government; the antiquarian value being four pounds the ounce, or even more, if the article is of special rarity or beauty. According to the best Irish authorities, there is proof that the gold mines of Wicklow were worked fully three thousand years ago. They were well known to the people, and from the quantity of the metal found in the plain of the Liffey, the men of Leinster were anciently styled 'The Lagenians of the Gold.'

Gold is still found in Wicklow, but the mines are not worked, as the result was not considered equal to the cost of working; yet in 1796, an experiment having been made, ten thousand pounds' worth of the precious metal was procured in a few weeks from one of the Wicklow mines, and in the very place where, according to the old annalists, gold was first smelted and fashioned into ornaments. Besides Wicklow, there are several other auriferous districts in Ireland; Wexford, Dublin, Kildare, Antrim, and Londonderry have all produced gold, and many places are associated with the word Oir (gold) from the quantity found there, either unwrought or manufactured. Thus in Kerry there is a place called Dun-an-oir, the Fort of the Gold, from the number of gold ornaments found secreted in one hoard, deep in the ground.

Irish gold in its native state is generally found in grains or nodules, frequently on the surface, washed down by the mountain streams and rivers. It is always slightly alloyed with silver and copper. The silver was much used by the ancient artificers, and brooches were made of thin plates of gold hammered down on a basis of silver. A slight artificial alloy of silver or copper was also often used by the ancient goldsmiths to produce the color required for manufactured ornaments, silver giving a pale hue, while the admixture of copper produced what is called 'the red gold.' Renewed efforts will probably now be made to work the gold districts of Ireland, the attention of the Empire having been recently aroused to the value and importance of native gold by the interesting and very successful explorations in Wales. Only a year ago operations were commenced in Merionethshire, through the influence and generous aid of Mr. Pritchard Morgan, the great Australian capitalist; it being well known that gold existed there, and had been worked in former times.

The result has been most encouraging; for within four months above four thousand ounces of gold were obtained by the miners; the value being over fourteen thousand pounds. Mr. Pritchard Morgan is now turning his attention to Ireland, and has already obtained Crown leases of fifty-four square miles of land in Wicklow, which he proposes working for gold, being convinced that with capital and proper machinery the Irish gold districts can still be worked with great commercial profit; but as a preliminary step, he is anxious that an influential gold mining company should be formed, as in Wales, without delay, to supply the necessary funds, and to direct and secure the success of the explorations. Thus a rich source of wealth, and a new and profitable industry, may be opened to the Irish people to stimulate their energies, and to send a tide of fresh activity through the land.

Primitive Man

No matter how far civilization may have progressed in any country during the long lapse of ages, yet the beginning of the life of humanity was simple and uniform throughout the entire world. Man formed implements to aid his own natural force, which is limited, and by their aid he has gradually made it almost infinite. To provide for his daily subsistence, he had to invent the ax, the wedge, the bow, the canoe, and if he had not made tools to help himself to sustain life, he would have remained far inferior to the animal creation in power and resources, though they are only guided by instinct.

Primitive man picked up the hardest flints,, struck them together and produced fire. Then he shaped and fashioned the flint chips by the aid of each other, and with these first rude elements of human power he could hew wood, dig the ground, kill his prey, and make war, or defend himself from. other tribes.

The flint ax was the first symbol in the history of humanity, it is contemporary with the mastodon, and is the oldest record of human work to be found on the face of the globe. There is nothing more ancient than this tool, and nothing more humble; yet archaeologists can read the history of the primal race by it, as the astronomers calculate the orbit of a planet from measuring an arc of the circle. The first chapter in human life was the Age of Stone; the beginning of all things; when men dwelt in caves, and with their implements of flint or wood slew the wild animals for food and made clothing of the skins, deftly sewn together with thongs, using a fish bone for a needle; or wove tunics of plaited rushes, and cut their moccasins out of untanned hide, sewn in a like manner with the sinews of animals. But primitive man had also abundance of oysters for his sustenance, as has been proved by the enormous mounds of oyster-shells still existing in Denmark, among which may be sometimes found, even now, the flint knives used by the cave-men for opening the nutritive bivalve.

The Age of Stone, when men cleared a path through the central forests of Europe with their stone axes, and fought for existence with the bear and the hyena, may have lasted for countless ages, while the world was preparing for the Adamic race- the last and highest that has yet appeared on earth; but it seems almost certain that the cave-men, the antediluvian or pre-Adamic race, never attained to a more advanced grade, for no evidence of a knowledge of metals has been found among their remains.

Metal, for the most part, remains hidden in the earth and the rocks, and cannot be used without much, labor and dexterous manipulation; but stone lies at the feet of man, before his eyes, and by the simplest effort can be made into a tool or a weapon, from the rudest hatchet to the highly finished flint implement which has received the modern name of celt, from celtis, a chisel, though some people erroneously imagine from the word that the implement owed its origin to the Celtic race. But the Celtic people, from whom the Irish are descended, are infinitely dissevered from the lower primal race of the cave-men, and did not follow in their track till perhaps a thousand years after the men of the Stone Age had spread over the world and were passing into oblivion. The Celts, when they first reached the West of Europe from their Eastern home, were to a certain degree advanced in culture, and had the knowledge of metals, at least of copper, which in time they learned to combine with tin, and thus formed the beautiful bronze weapons and tools, of which so many hundreds have been found in Ireland, unsurpassed in any modern work for the brilliancy and beauty of the metal, which shines like burnished gold.

The Celts found the stone hatchet in the hands of the indigenous race, and adopted the form which they reproduced in bronze, and added to the weapons and tools they had already in use. The first furrows of civilization were traced and dug by the primitive man with his rude stone implements and without the aid of metal; but the higher race, the Adamic, seems, if we trust the Bible, to have had a knowledge of metals from the very beginning, and the Age of Copper was the first in date of the two great metallic ages, copper being comparatively easy to extract and to work. The Celts of Ireland used it for their weapons from the earliest dawn of history, and it was the first metal which became of importance to man, being smelted without difficulty, and even hammered into shape easily in its native condition. But finally, brass, like the stone that preceded it, gave place to a still more powerful metal, and the Age of Iron succeeded. This metal produced an immense revolution in the world, and is the source of all the higher developments of human industry, for its power is illimitable and its uses are infinite; and modern life and civilization date from the knowledge and employment of iron beyond that of any other metal.

Thus, in the history of humanity, the law may be formulated- the Age of Stone first, the Age of Iron last, the Age of Brass intermediate and transitional. And legend and mythology have a certain basis of truth when they divide the epochs of the world into the Age of Gold, of Brass, and of Iron. For the knowledge of gold certainly preceded that of all other metals. As Sir John Lubbock remarks in his important and valuable work, 'Prehistoric Times': "Gold was the metal which no doubt first attracted the attention of man, as it is often found on the surface, and in many rivers, and by its bright color would certainly prove attractive even to the rudest savage tribes, who instinctively love color and personal decoration." Silver was not in use until long after gold, and was preceded by both copper and tin; but gold was often used in its crude state for ornamental purposes by savage tribes, though it never was of importance to human life for industrial purposes. A few years ago a cave was discovered in Spain containing several skeletons, all clothed in tunics of woven rushes, but decorated on the neck and arms with bracelets and collars of crude gold pressed into shape, and one skeleton, who, perhaps, was the king or chief, wore in addition a circlet of gold round the head- but no gold has been discovered as yet in Ireland belonging to the Stone Age.

The New Races

The cave-men, who had originally made the world their own, and overspread the whole earth, seem at last to have entirely passed away, having fulfilled their mission, as pioneers of the higher humanity that was to come; and they finally became extinct, along with the mammoth and the mastodon, and the great Cervus Megaceros of Ireland, and the many other giants of land and sea, that were contemporary with the rudimentary humanity of the first ages of life. So when the world was sufficiently prepared for the new race, the men of the Stone Age died out, leaving no descendants, and no other evidence of their existence save the silent but eternal symbols of stone, by which we can see how they lived and worked, and had their being, and take the measure of their mental standard, which, though the lowest of the human types, yet was not without some instincts of art and design, for they drew rude sketches on the walls of their caves, and their weapons had often. a rude ornamentation, the product perhaps of their leisure hours.

The races that followed to people the world belonged to a new creation, a higher humanity; and to them we owe all, the great representatives of mankind in history, and all the existing peoples of the earth. Chief among them may be named the Semitic, Teutonic, and the Celtic races- the Semite being always eminent for religion; the Teuton for conquest, rule, and power; and the Celt for art and intellect. The Celtic race that founded our own Irish nation, and from whom the Irish nature obtains all its peculiar characteristics, was the first to bring culture to Ireland, architecture, the symbols of writing, and the arts of weaving and metal work, along with a code of laws that trained the people to a sense of right and justice. Intellect among them was deemed worthy of the highest honor; and while all Europe lay in darkness, the Celts of Ireland in the early Christian centuries were distinguished for their love of art and learning, and sent forth from their schools many a man of eminence to carry the torch of light through the world; and to this day in all the highest illustrations of intellect in Europe can be traced a strain of the Celtic blood.

ANCIENT CURES, CHARMS, AND USAGES OF IRELAND

It is remarkable that through all the lapse of ages, the distinctive characteristics of a race never change or alter. The Semite is still the priest, the Teuton the warrior, and the Celt the artist and poet of the world. Three thousand years may have passed by, yet the Semitic race stands, as of old, at the head of the highest religious code and doctrine. The Teuton has never ceased going forth conquering and to conquer, till nearly the whole world is now under his sway; and the Celt (with whom we Irish have a living affinity), is still the passionate poet and orator, the centrifugal force of the human polity, ever sending forth a rush of new thought into the world, to kindle as with light and flame the hopes and aspirations of oppressed peoples and nations, and to arouse their energies for the holy war against wrong, and for the sublime cause of human right.

THE AMERICAN IRISH

The Irish of Today

The record of Irish wrong is now, perhaps, scarcely remembered by the nation whose struggles for conquest so long made Ireland a land of mourning and woe; but the tale still lives in Irish hearts with enduring vitality. Every century has witnessed some fierce effort to throw off the foreign yoke, and every generation adds new names to the long roll of martyrs and victims doomed to suffer for the vain but beautiful dream of national independence. Exile, confiscation, the prison, and the scaffold form the leading chapters of Irish history, even to our own day- an endless martyrology written in tears and blood.

Yet, some good has come of the evil. Many holy and sacred things spring up in a nation's soul from the seed sown by persecution. Suffering purifies and refines, and a people learns the value of coherence and unity mainly through oppression. There is also something ennobling in the love of an object out of self, in the devotion to an abstraction called Country; in this dream of freedom, with all the word means- dignity, honor, self-reverence, and self-respect. It will be a sad day, perhaps, for the higher national life when Ireland has no more dreams, and the country no more martyrs, for then an ideal will have passed out of the life of the people, and a nation without an ideal aim on which to concentrate the passions, soon becomes hopelessly materialized, inarticulate, and dull. The subtle, spiritual fancies, and the finer issues of human feeling, are stifled by the sensuous, selfish enjoyment of the actual and the present; and nations, as well as individuals, become hard and cold, without the divine impulse of sacrifice and self-abnegation. To the impassioned nationality of the Irish, with its large indefiniteness of aim and instincts of resistance, may be also due much of the fervor of Irish eloquence. All oppressed nations are eloquent. When laws forbid a people to arm, they can only speak or sing.

Words become their weapons, and the Irish armory is always bright and burning. Nationality, this dream of an ideal future, illumines their poetry and oratory, their music and song, with a vague splendor of passion and pathos, and preserves even the common speech and popular literature of the people from the coarseness and vulgarity so obtrusively characteristic of the English lower classes.

Ireland, then, has some compensation for her suffering; many fine-toned chords in the nature of her people, a gentle courtesy of manner that is almost reverential, and a power of winning sympathy and love which the stolid English organization, with its plethoric prosperity and self-centered egotism, is entirely without. It is remarkable, also, that wherever the Irish are located in other lands, they never forget the old country. It is still the Mecca to which their eyes are ever turned. Exile even seems to intensify their feelings, and the fearless oratory of passion glows with a fervor that would be impossible in the police-ruled country at home. In America, more especially, free speech knows no limit with regard to the past and future of Ireland. Irish festivals are celebrated there with words that clang like swords, while memorial rituals keep the martyrs of freedom for ever living before the eyes of the people. Armed clubs are named after the chief leaders of Irish revolt, and solemn processions mark the anniversary of each national tragedy, for there are no triumphs to record in Irish history.

The Greeks of old wrote the names of their heroes in letters of gold upon the walls of their temples; the Irish must search for the names of their heroes on the walls of a prison. This consecration of revolt, this canonization of the victims of rebellion, has a powerful influence on the young generation of American Irish. It kindles a bitter and deathless indignation in their hearts, and, like a warm gulf stream, the tide of their passion surges across the Atlantic to raise the temperature at home to the revolutionary heat, which, in these days, generally culminates in the endeavor to found a Republic. It is singular that the Irish may live for years in England, yet they never acquire the English manner- calm, grave, and self-possessed; nor the English habits of order and routine; nor even the English accent- while in America they rapidly become Americanized, bold in speech, audacious in enterprise, self-asserting in manner, and, above all, Republican in sentiment.

No Irishman returns from America loyal to Monarchy. On the contrary, he laughs to scorn the old bonds of servile feudalism, with all its superstitions of class worship; and his opinions soon gain many followers. The American flag holds the place of honor at all popular demonstrations in Ireland, and is always greeted with enthusiastic cheers, while the flag of England is nowhere seen. (It was the American flag that waved over the liberated Fenian prisoners during the great torchlight procession in Dublin to welcome their return. The English flag was not visible anywhere.)

These are some of the outward and visible signs of the rapid spread of American influence and Republican tendencies among the Irish people,, and it is a natural result, considering the incessant intercourse, and the strong relationship existing between Ireland and America. Tear by year Ireland sends forth thousands of her people in the emigrant ships, like outcast weeds to be flung on the shores of America, a helpless crowd of crushed, dispirited, unlettered peasants; slaves and serfs -who have never even known their rights as freemen, dulled by want, oppression, and despair; speaking, perhaps, no language save the ancient tongue of the primitive Celt, through which no new light of thought has flashed for a thousand years, seeing nothing, knowing nothing in all God's great universe save the two awful and irresistible forces that for them rule earth and heaven, the landlord and the priest.

Silent and troubled, with the scared, sad look of the hunted deer, they gather on the beach amid the wild cries of their kindred, and sail away in the exile ship, with all its unknown horrors, to the unknown land beyond the sea, as if they were passing to another life through the gates of death. But, in the next decade the children of these serfs of the desolated lives, the bewildered brain, and the darkened soul, spring up at once to the level of the nineteenth century- ardent in purpose, fearless in word, eager for action, and filled with a glowing ambition to scale those heights which under a Republic are accessible to all who have intellect and daring. The past is not forgotten, but they stand on it as on a pedestal, from whence they take a wider survey of their position, and recognize the truth at last that life means something more to man than mere passive endurance of the negation of all things that build up a nation, or a human soul. They are no longer helpless, incoherent masses of ignorant and unorganized men, waifs driven by the storm-winds of despair, with only bitter memories, or vengeful hopes to guide, that, like torches held over an abyss by an uncertain hand, too often lead but to dismay and ruin.

The American Irish are the opposite of all this. They receive a soldier's training, with full privileges of freemen and citizens. They are educated and organized; important by their numbers, and by that ready talent and indomitable spirit which is rapidly gaining for them the highest positions as statesmen, generals, orators, writers, and journalists in the States.

Laws and Governments have an immense influence upon the moral nature of a people, and help to create a national character as much, or even more, than the ethnic elements out of which a nation is formed. Under a Republic, men acquire those noble qualities of self-reverence, self-respect, and personal dignity, rarely found among oppressed races; and the Irish nature, so long trodden down and humbled, and made almost abjectly servile through fear and coercion and penal laws, gains a new force and sense of strength under Republican teaching that is like an awakening from a death sleep. The vastness of America, the gigantic enterprise, the infinite extent of her resources, the boundless wealth waiting on every side for the skillful hand and the energetic brain, have a peculiarly stimulating effect upon the multitudes who have quit a country where energy finds no work for hand or brain, and intellect has neither honor nor reward. The lassitude and languor induced by the utter stagnation of all things at home is thrown off, and men begin to feel that if they have the gifts to win success, they have also a right to share those splendid rewards which under a Monarchy are reserved almost exclusively for a favored few, but which a Republic offers freely to all. And the American Irish are now powerful enough to command success. They have become a great and mighty people in the land of their adoption- a nation greater than the nation at home. There are twice as many Irish now in America as there are in Ireland. They form a third of the population of all the great cities, and are banded together in one powerful organization by race, religion, memory, and hopes. They have also one aim, which is to create a new era in the history of Ireland. This is the fanaticism of their lives- but they bide their time; the individual dies, the nation lives and waits. The English sneer down the idea, yet nothing will eradicate the splendid dream from the Celtic imagination that some day the Irish race will be powerful enough to recross the Atlantic with ships and arms and money, overthrow English rule, and annex Ireland to the great Federal Republic under the Stars and Stripes. And it must be confessed that the project is not wholly improbable or impossible, should there be some new arrangement of the nationalities of the world, for America needs a standpoint in Europe, and Ireland would form a capital Atrium for the unresting, eternally moving masses of the American people, who, having already swept along the whole coast of the Pacific, will soon be surging across the Atlantic to seek new homes. Indeed the subject has already been openly discussed, and even a suggestion offered that America should purchase Ireland from the English Government in a peaceable, orderly way; for considering what a thorn in the flesh the Green Isle has ever been to England, the severance, it is thought, might be made without much grief on either side. Meanwhile, the American Irish boast of their ten millions, all ready to pour across the Atlantic when the fitting moment comes in which they can reconstruct their ancient motherland upon the newest Republican principles.

We are accustomed to think of Ireland as only a nation of five millions, according to home statistics and census reports; but, including Australia with America, the Irish may be counted at eighteen or twenty millions; and in case of some violent European complication, or of war between England and the United States, it may be interesting to speculate on which side these millions would range themselves. Gratitude would bind them to America; they could never fight against the flag that sheltered them in their adversity, when evil laws and bitter tyranny forced them to abandon their own unhappy country; and they could scarcely be expected to show an enthusiastic desire to support England even at the sacrifice of their lives.

So tremendous a catastrophe, however, as war between England and the States will probably never happen, but revolutions may come silently and with spirit steps. Such a revolution, silent gradual, but certain, is now going on in the Irish mind abroad and at home, and some day the new ideas will find visible expression in perhaps a higher national life than any Ireland has yet known. Education will create a new history; it is the force that above all others molds the destiny of a people, and teaches them how to utilize their chances and opportunities. Hitherto the Irish have groped blindly after their ideal, which is National Independence- this is the magic phrase that binds them together as one people all over the world, as if it symbolized a religion; and if they have striven for it through seven centuries of darkness and disorganization, they are not likely to give it up now in this nineteenth century, when Liberty from the shores of America holds high her torch for men to read their rights by; and America has, in an especial manner, constituted herself the teacher of the Irish people. Lectures upon Irish history, poetry, oratory, and all that illustrates the genius, sufferings, wrongs, and destiny of the Irish, are the most popular of all subjects throughout the States, and attract eager and sympathetic crowds, for, strange to say, these subjects have also the additional charm of novelty. The Irish people are reared upon traditions, but have little accurate knowledge of their own history, while the upper classes are notoriously ignorant of it, with the exception of a few learned Academicians who study it curiously, as they do the Vedas, for mere ethnological or philological purposes.

ANCIENT CURES, CHARMS, AND USAGES OF IRELAND

The reason of this national ignorance is simply that Irish history is not taught in any of the schools? of Ireland; not in the National schools, nor the endowed schools, nor is it included in the course at the Queen's Colleges or the Dublin University, to qualify for a degree. In Irish education, Irish history is steadily ignored by schools, academies, and colleges, a national annihilation that probably could find no counterpart in all the rest of Europe. Irish children may recite the kings of the Heptarchy, or the causes of the Punic Wars, but of the long, heroic struggles of their forefathers against foreign domination, they are taught never a word.

Naturally, the object of an alien Government was to extinguish the idea of a country, to degrade and obliterate heroic memories, to brand a patriot as a traitor, and nationality as treason; and in this manner the pride, self-respect, and self-reliance of the Irish people have been slowly murdered through the centuries- for strong and noble qualities like these are only found among a people who are taught the dignity of nationhood, and to reverence the men of their race who have toiled, and fought, and suffered for some great idea, or some sublime word. America, however, fully responds to the eager desire of the Irish among them for fuller knowledge and clearer light. Many influential journals are almost wholly devoted to Irish subjects, and the past and future of Ireland are discussed with a fearless audacity unknown here; for, as Emerson remarks: "There is a boundless freedom in the States, and people have been put to death in other countries for uttering what are but the commonplaces of American writers." One of the best of these journals is The Boston Pilot, edited by an Irishman, John Boyle O'Reilly, the distinguished author of 'Songs from the Southern Seas,' a series of wild, fierce tales of adventure, remarkable for startling originality of conception, nervous language, and a full flow of sonorous harmonies in the versification. Another journal of considerable critical ability. The New York Nation, is also edited by an Irishman, Mr. Grodkin, son of the author of 'Ireland and her Churches,' and other works. The Irish World, the favorite organ of the ultra-democratic party, has a fiercer inspiration, and openly advocates an armed invasion of Ireland, and the redistribution of all the confiscated estates. This journal is indeed so violently anti-English, and the illustrations are so bitterly sarcastic on the English Court (although with none of the revolting ribaldry permitted to appear in some of the London papers), that recently it has been stopped at the Irish Post Office, and the priesthood discourage its circulation among the people. It is, however, extremely popular with the extreme section of the American Irish, and is held to be a true exponent of their views. Among the many works issued by the American press on Irish subjects, the most recent, and by far the most important, is the 'History of the Successive Confiscations of Ireland,' by Mr. Amory, including lists of the families whose estates were seized and divided among the English adventurers. ('The Transfer of Erin,' by Thomas C. Amory, Lippencott & Co, Philadelphia 1877.) The work has excited great attention in America, for descendants of all these families may be found in the States, and they are proud of their kinship with the old historic clans. (An immense interest has been recently manifested in America on the subject of family history. Since the close of the war people have had little to do, and so have taken to heraldry, and we may soon expect a Columbian King-at-arms, and an American Debrett.) Mr. Amory, the author, an American of distinguished position, influence, and wealth, whose opinion is of the highest value, writes with much kindly feeling of the Irish, yet with fairness and moderation, while he states the truth boldly at the same time, with respect to English policy, as only an American may dare to do. "If Ireland," he says, "still remains turbulent and disaffected, the fault is due to England, who never strove to gain the love of the people, but crushed, and despoiled, and exterminated in place of affiliating... Had Irishmen," he continues, "been left lords of their own lands, and not made bondsmen to strangers, they would have been the honor and safety of the united realm, and proved themselves, as they are in America, an intelligent, thrifty, law abiding, brave, generous, and noble-hearted people."

And when the Irish have shown themselves so worthy of freedom, he considers it "base and unjust in the highest degree for English writers to pursue them across the Atlantic, casting obloquy on their nation, their history, and their traditions, with the sole aim apparently of lowering them in the eyes of the people who shelter and protect them."

In the interest, therefore, of fair play, he undertook the work "to show the true nature of English rule from which sprang all the evils of Irish destiny." And he has accomplished his task with great ability. Every page shows careful and extensive reading, and patient study of the involved and complicated details of Irish history, along with a generous, high-spirited feeling towards Ireland, that contrasts very favorably with the usual tone of English writers on the same subject. In the early portion of the 'History,' he chiefly follows 'the Four Masters,' but he has also amassed material from many other sources, ancient and modern, so that his volume is really a condensed history of Ireland down to the time of Elizabeth, when the last gleam of independent sovereignty died out with the submission of the great O'Neill, after a ceaseless war of four hundred years between the two races. A second volume will tell the story of Irish confiscations from James I. to Cromwell and William of the Boyne; after which the gloom of the penal laws settled on the country, and the Irish had no more land to be confiscated, nor even a legal right to hold any land on their own soil. "For a far less amount of wrong," Mr. Amory remarks, "the Americans cast off the English yoke for ever, and proclaimed independence."

The early portion of Irish history is passed over slightly,

for there were no confiscations prior to the Norman invasion. The land belonged to the clan, and the goods of life were abundant and shared by all alike. The condition of the Irish people was better a thousand years ago than it is now; the progress of civilization makes the rich richer, but the poor poorer. (A thousand years ago the people of Ireland had their share in the cattle of the plains, the salmon of the rivers, and the deer of the forest; now the railroads carry off all the produce of land and rivers for export. The great proprietors in consequence grow wealthy, but the peasants are reduced to the level of a root-eating people, and never taste meat but twice a year- at Christmas and Easter.) They seem to have lived happily in those primitive days, with music and song and cosherings and feastings, where they drank at their banquets of "the best seven sorts of wine," and never a care troubled them save an occasional brush with the Danes, or with each other, to keep their shields bright and their swords clean. Nor were they deficient in artistic culture; their golden diadems, torques, bracelets, and other personal ornaments were costly and splendid, and evinced a skill in workmanship rarely equaled in this day. Like the Greeks, they prized highly personal gifts, and their kings were chosen for their stature, strength, and beauty. Courage they esteemed as one of the noblest virtues, and victory the highest glory. "What do you desire?" asked Saint Bridget of a great chief. "Shall I pray that the crown may never depart from your race, and that your soul may find rest in heaven?"

"I care not for heaven," he answered, "of which I know nothing, but for long life in this world, in which I greatly delight, and for victory over my enemies." And Saint Patrick, having questioned the king on the eve of battle: "Which will you have- for my prayers cures powerful- defeat today and heaven for ever, or victory and hell?" received the emphatic answer, "Hell to all eternity; so the victory is mine today in the battle!"

ANCIENT CURES, CHARMS, AND USAGES OF IRELAND

When the Normans came, the Irish were no rude barbarians, as some English writers have endeavored to represent them. They had a Christian civilization of seven centuries; a learned priesthood, honored throughout Europe; colleges for instruction, the resort of many Saxon princes; musicians eminent in their art above all others and a code of wise, just laws, including evidences of much tender feeling towards the weak and helpless. Even in the pagan time a queen of Ireland erected a hospital near her own royal residence for the sick and those wounded in battle, and called it 'The House of Sorrow.' The many stately abbeys, the sculptured crosses, the illuminated manuscripts (which to the Normans seemed the work of angels) attest their wonderful sense of symmetry and beauty, and their reverence for all things pertaining to religion; while evidences of a still older art and culture exist in those mystic towers which Giraldus Cambrensis gazed upon with awe and wonder above six centuries ago, and which happily, though volumes have been written on the subject, still remain inscrutable, for nothing could be more revolting to the imaginative mind than the satisfactory solution of a world-old mystery.

Farther back, even in the very night of time, are the sepulchers of the Boyne, and the Cyclopean Temple of New Grange, relics of the same mighty race that dwelt on the Argive plain, and were the Cyclopean builders of Mycenae. Rude in art, but powerful in strength, their tombs stand to this day in all their awful and majestic grandeur in Ireland as in Greece, memorials of the great, silent race, that had no literature and no alphabet, but whose colossal symbols of expression were temples and tombs.

The Celts in many things have a strong affinity with the Greeks, the highest honors were given to learning and poetry, and their music had the same subtle power ascribed to the Dorian measure, which had "such strange influence over the human soul, that the bards were often summoned to heal feuds by their divine harmony."

A people of this sensitive temperament, proud, passionate, and warlike, accustomed to think greatly of their race, who had owned the soil for nearly two thousand years before the coming of the Normans, and had never endured the yoke of the Caesars, nor the presence of a foreign enemy, save the pirate Danes of the coasts, was ill-fitted to bear the hard, insulting tyranny of English rule. The stolid Saxons had a different temperament, they were rapidly crushed, and humbled, and made the serfs of their Norman masters; and after a while they patiently accepted their fate, and became the traders, and toilers, and factory hands of the Empire, no man pitying them. It was evident that nature meant them for a destiny of inferiority, for a servile race, and so they have remained ever since, emphatically 'the lower classes' of England.

The Celts, on the contrary, with their Greek nature, love glory, and beauty, and distinction, everything that is free and splendid, but they hate toil and despise trade. They were made for warriors and orators, for a life of excitement and daring, lit by swift impulses, fast and fiery as electric flashes. They will do anything for love or fame. They adore a hero, but they will never tamely submit to coercion, injustice, and a position of inferiority, like the apathetic, dull-brained Saxon.

It would indeed be impossible to find natures more entirely antagonistic than the Saxon and the Celt. The English live under method and rule laboriously and industriously, without excitement or ambition, and will even bear oppression, so as a chance of gain comes with it. They will manufacture muskets for their own country, or for the foreign army that fights against England, with equal readiness, and dispassionate commercial calm; and they will shout for war with the Turk or the Christian, or against them, not for the sake of God, but for the sake of cotton. But of all races the Celt is the most easily led by the affections. If the people believe that their popular hero really loves Ireland, they would sacrifice their lives for him. The English are grateful for benefits to self, the Irish are grateful for sympathy with their country. When they say of a man, "He died for Ireland," the voice is low and tender, as if they spoke of the passion of Christ. The great mistake of England was not trying to gain the love of this people. The Irish demand some visible personal object for their homage and devotion, but England's rule was only known to them through cruel Acts of Parliament, and to her demand for 'gratitude' they might have answered:

"We, for all our good things, have at your hands-
Death, barrenness, child slaughter, curses, cares,
Sea leaguer, and land shipwreck, which of these
Which shall we first give thanks for?"

The Irish are naturally loyal, with an almost oriental abnegation of self, to those they love; but the English never cultivated their affection, and never comprehended the deeply reverential Irish nature, so full of passionate fanaticism, that sympathy with their ideal, whatever that may be, whether in politics or religion, is more to them than if gold were showered upon their path; but as they never received sympathy or affection, but only taunts, insults, and penal laws, the history of Ireland, from the fatal year 1172 to the present hour, is the saddest in Europe.

Yet the first invaders conquered more through love than war. The Normans were a fine, brave, high-spirited race, one of the leonine races with firm noses, as Victor Hugo describes them, destined to conquer. They intermarried rapidly with the royal families of Ireland, and thus immense estates passed into their hands, many of which are held by their descendants to this day. The five daughters of Isabel, grand-daughter of King Dermot Mac-Murrough, had each a county for her dower ; they all wedded English nobles, and it is remarkable that to this line can be traced all the highest names in the English peerage, the royal family of England, and, through the Stuarts, all the leading crowned heads of Europe.

The Norman Irish, the descendants of these mixed marriages, grew into a splendid and powerful race, the Geraldines at their head. Queen Elizabeth came of this blood through her mother and the Ormonds, indeed, Mr. Hepworth Dixon imputes the fascinations of Anne Boleyn to this Irish strain; and the Irish gradually came to love these Norman nobles who lived among them, adopted their speech and dress, and often fought with the clans against England. But these strong bonds of friendship soon excited the jealousy of the English kings, and it is a singular fact that the first coercion laws in Ireland were enacted to break this amity between the two races. Marriage was strictly forbidden with the Irish, and fosterage- for the children grew so fond of their foster kindred, that they often refused to leave them, and renouncing allegiance to England, adopted the Irish mode of life and dress. But no laws were found adequate to prevent intermarriage. Even Spenser, the poet, when he came over to receive his three thousand, acres of the forfeited estates, took to wife an Irish girl, whose portrait he has sketched so prettily in the 'Epithalamium'; and all Cromwell's troopers, when they settled down with their land warrants, married Irishwomen, despite the severest penalties. Then a new danger alarmed England, for the children of these marriages spoke nothing but Irish, and complaints were made by the officials that the English tongue was almost dying out in Ireland; further efforts were made in consequence to force the English settlers to put away their Irish wives, but in vain.

Thus a second mixed race sprang up in Ireland, still

known as 'the Cromwellian Irish,' strong Protestants, but Liberal in politics, and rather Republican in theory. Meanwhile the Irish disdained to use the language of the invaders, or adopt their dress, for 'the tribes of Erin ever hated foreign modes.' The English kings sometimes sent over presents of costly robes to the great chieftains, but they refused to wear them; and Shane O'Neill appeared at the Court of Queen Elizabeth in the long flowing yellow mantle, brooched with gold, after the Irish fashion, and addressed her Majesty in Irish, which she was ungracious enough to say resembled "the howling of a dog."

When asked to confer in English with the Commissioners, he replied, indignantly: "What! shall an O'Neill writhe his mouth in clattering English?" The husband of Grana-Uaile, a De Burgho, could speak French, and Latin, and Irish, but no English; and one frequently reads in the annals of some Norman noble, who swore brotherhood with an Irish chieftain, and assumed the Irish dress, and Irish speech, in sign of friendship. In order therefore to crush more completely the tendency to union between the two races, drawn together by sentiments of chivalry and love, a policy of the most insulting degradation was adopted towards the Irish of the Pale. They were forced to give up their old historic names, and assume hideous and unmeaning surnames, from colors, as black, white, gray, green, brown; or from fishes, as salmon, cod, haddock, plaice, and every other stupid appellation that malice could invent, and by which the old associations of noble descent might be obliterated. They were also excluded from all places of trust and honor; the son had to follow his father's trade, lest by some chance he should rise in the social scale, and at all times it seems to have been held a praiseworthy act to kill an Irishman, without let or hindrance, fear of law, or punishment of the slayer. The Norman nobles who sided with the clans were also persecuted, and great portions of their estates were given over to a new lot of English colonists less friendly to the Irish. The Geraldines especially, being the most powerful, were treated with most severity. In the reign of Henry VIII., six nobles of the Geraldines were executed in London for aiding rebellion among the Irish, but even this bitter vengeance could not quench their national zeal. From Silken Thomas to the fated and interesting Lord Edward Fitzgerald, the great house of Kildare has always been on the side of the Irish nation.

The war of races lasted without intermission for four hundred years, dating from the invasion until the fall of O'Neill, Earl of Tyrone, the last independent prince of Ulster. (The Rev. C.P. Meehan has graphically described this memorable epoch of Irish history in his admirable volume entitled, 'The Flight of the Earls.') Then followed the still fiercer war of religions, which has not even yet ended. Queen Elizabeth resolved that the Irish should become Protestant, and burnings, massacres, and devastation were the persuasive means employed.

All who would not conform were driven from their homes, and left to perish in the bogs and woods where they tried to find a shelter. All the South was confiscated and divided among a set of Protestant English adventurers. The Irish were cast forth to die, and the horrible work of destruction went on until even the Queen complained that she would soon reign only over ashes and corpses. Spenser, the poet, has left a vivid description of the state of Ireland at that time. He describes the land as 'the fairest upon earth,' but the people wandered about like ghosts from the grave, houseless and starving, and all the roads were strewn with the unburied dead. When King James came to the throne the Irish had a gleam of hope. He was a Stuart of the line of their ancient kings, and they looked for tenderness at his hands for the sake of his Catholic mother; but the hope was vain. The war of religions waxed fiercer, and the persecution was more bitter and cruel. Queen Elizabeth had confiscated the South; King James confiscated the North, and handed over the fishful rivers and broad lands of Ulster to the Worshipful Fishmongers of London, who rejoice in their possession even unto this day. And again, massacres, burnings, and devastation were the means employed to get rid of the unhappy natives of the soil. It was not wonderful that a terrible vendetta should be the result. In the memorable year 1641 the Irish rose en masse, headed by Lord Maguire, Earl of Enniskillen, with the avowed object of sweeping all the English out of the island at once, seizing Dublin Castle, and proclaiming a national independent Government.

But the project failed, as all projects against English power have failed in Ireland. Lord Maguire was captured and brought over to London for trial. He was but twenty-six (the leaders of revolutions are all young), and he met his fate with the calmness of a martyr for religion. When they teased him with taunts upon Romish doctrines, and advice to abjure them, he only answered; "I pray you, gentlemen, let me have peace that I may pray." He earnestly pleaded to be tried by his peers in deference to his rank, and to be beheaded in place of being hung; these requests were denied, and having been degraded from his title of Lord Enniskillen, which afterwards was conferred upon one of the Cole family, he was drawn on a sledge from the Tower through London, and on to Tyburn, where, being removed into a cart, he knelt down and prayed, awhile, and so was executed.(An interesting novel founded on the rising of 1641, entitled 'Tully Castle,' by Mr. Magennis, of Fermanagh, has recently appeared. The hero is Lord Maguire, and the trial scene and his tragic death are drawn with much power and minute accuracy of detail.) The war of religions went on with still increasing bitterness during the Republican period between the Irish, who held for King Charles, and the Parliamentary forces, until Cromwell himself at last appeared upon the scene, and stifled Royalists and Catholics alike in a bath of blood. South and North had already been confiscated. Cromwell completed the work by confiscating all the rest of Ireland. His policy was extermination, and this he carried out with a ruthless ferocity that has made his name eternally abhorred in Ireland. "The curse of Cromwell on you" is the bitterest malediction a peasant can utter even to this day.

The Irish were the Canaanites to be hewed down branch and root. Had the nation had but one neck he would have struck it off. The priests were massacred by hundreds, the nobles were driven into exile, the women and children were sold in thousands as slaves to the West India planters. The whole of the land was seized, and five million acres were parceled out by lot to his troops in payment of their arrears of pay. The bleakest portion of Connaught alone was reserved for the remnant of the Irish people amid the wild, treeless mountains of the West, and thither the fugitives were driven during all the rigors of winter, with orders not to approach within five miles of the sea under penalty of death- the object being to shut up the last survivors of the Irish nation from all intercourse with the world, and, if possible, to extirpate them wholly by famine and sickness.

One should read this tragic tale of the uprooting of a nation in Mr. Prendergast's great historic work, 'The Cromwellian Settlement of Ireland' (One of the most valuable contributions which this age has given to Irish history, and perfectly trustworthy, being compiled from authentic sources and State papers.) No nation ever endured greater horrors, and no people but the Irish could have survived them. The land remained untilled, the cattle and corn were destroyed, and food had to be imported from Wales for Cromwell's soldiery. A court-martial sat in St. Patrick's Cathedral, and all delinquents who refused to go to Connaught were hanged, with a placard on the breast, "for not transplanting." The corpses of the slain and the famine-struck were flung into the ditches; multitudes perished from want, and the roads were covered with the unburied dead. The wolves came down from the mountains in such numbers to seize their prey, that traveling became dangerous because of them. Then a price was set on the wolves and on the men who still wandered about the woods and bogs near their ancient homes- five pounds for the skin of a wolf, ten pounds for the head of an Irishman, even twenty pounds if he were distinguished; still the heads did not come in fast enough, and a free pardon was then offered to any Irishman who killed another and brought his head to claim the reward. At length Parliament interfered, with a suggestion that it were better not to extirpate the whole nation, but to leave some to till the ground, as the Commissioners reported that four-fifths of the richest land lay waste and uninhabited. The English had now been governing Ireland for five hundred years, and this was the result. The accession of James II., however, promised better times. He was a Stuart and a Catholic, and the Irish always clung with fatal fondness to the Stuart race, as being of their own blood. But loyalty had no better fate than disaffection. They had leagued with Spain for the sake of King Charles; they now leagued with France for the sake of King James. Cromwell avenged the first, and William of Orange the second attempt to support English royalty by foreign arms; and after the decisive conflict of 1688 a deeper darkness settled upon Ireland. The policy of Elizabeth and her successors was confiscation; that of Cromwell extermination, but the policy of King William, or rather of his Parliament, was degradation, for the penal laws meant social and moral death; and statesmen then sedulously set themselves the task of debasing a whole people below the level of humanity. As a hero, William loved heroism, and the splendid valor of the Irish, their devotion to their king, their country, and their faith filled him with wonder and admiration. "Give them any terms they ask," he wrote to his generals at Limerick. And when twenty thousand of the best and bravest in Ireland went forth from the surrendered city and ranged themselves under the French flag, to pass from thence into the armies of his hereditary foe, how bitterly he regretted that such men should be driven into exile, or degraded to slaves if they remained at home. Earnestly he offered them everything men naturally desire- rank, wealth, a position as high in his army as they held in their own, if they would only enter his service. But the Irish heeded not; they knelt down reverently to kiss the Irish soil for a last farewell, and then passed on to the ships amid such lamentations as never were heard before in Ireland, and sailed away from their native land never to behold it more. ('The History of the Irish Brigade,' by Mr. O'Callaghan, gives a full account of the fate and fortune of these distinguished Irishmen and their descendants. Many of them founded noble families on the Continent, as the MacMahons of Prance, the O'Donnells of Spain, the Nugents, Taaffes, and O'Reillys of Austria, and many others.)

The laws of William's Parliament were cruel, but those of Queen Anne were ferocious. No other nation ever invented a code so fitted to destroy both soul and body. The son was set against the father, brother against brother, for the law decreed that the informer and betrayer should be rewarded with the estates and property of his victim. During the whole of the eighteenth century this atrocious code was endured by 'the Irish without any open revolt; but at last the bitter indignation of the people burst forth in the great rebellion of 1798- a movement, strange to say, which originated with the Presbyterians of Ulster, the descendants of the Scotch settlers of King James. Their object at first was simply to repeal the infamous penal laws, but gradually the organization became Republican under French influence, and the leadership of the fated Lord Edward Fitzgerald. How the rebellion was put down is still fresh in the minds of the people, for the generation is not yet extinct whose fathers witnessed the atrocities practiced.

The pitch cap was the favorite amusement of the English soldiery; piles of these caps were kept in readiness at the barracks, and when filled with burning pitch one was pressed tightly on the head of the victim, who, half-blinded and maddened by the agony, was then turned out to run the gauntlet of his savage tormentors until he dropped dead amid their shouts of ferocious laughter. Gunpowder was rubbed into the hair and then set on fire; the ears were cut off, priests and gentlemen of station were half hung to extort information.

Irish vengeance in return was often fierce and terrible, but deliberate torture does not seem to have been practiced at the rebel camp, and many impulsive acts of generosity in saving life are recorded of the insurgents. (On the day the rebels entered Wexford, the rector, Archdeacon Elgee, my grandfather, assembled a few of his parishioners in the church to partake of the sacrament together, knowing that a dreadful death awaited them. On his return, the rebels were already forcing their way into his house; they seized him, and the pikes were already at his breast, when a man stepped forth and told of some great act of kindness which, the Archdeacon had shown his family. In an instant the feeling changed, and the leader gave orders that the Archdeacon and all that belonged to him should be held safe from harm. A rebel guard was set over his house and not a single act of violence was permitted. But that same evening all the leading gentlemen of the town were dragged from their houses and piked by the rebels upon Wexford Bridge.)

At length '98 was put down; seventy thousand Irish lay dead, but the penal laws remained unchanged. The Irish Parliament at last began seriously to consider the disaffected state of the nation. Splendid men of genius and high purpose rose up to denounce wrong, injustice, and tyranny and the most magnificent advocacy of a people's rights ever uttered was heard in the Irish Parliament just before its fall. But the answer England gave to the noble appeal of the Irish patriots was brief and decisive; she simply annihilated the Parliament, and the voices of the prophets of freedom were heard no more.

ANCIENT CURES, CHARMS, AND USAGES OF IRELAND

The degradation of Ireland was now complete. After the Union, the palaces of the nobles were left desolate; wealth, spirit, enterprise, all the brilliancy of social and intellectual life vanished from the capital; the various trades died out one by one; literature became extinct; the publishing trade, once so vigorous and flourishing, almost entirely disappeared; the currents of thought and energy set to London, and have continued to flow there ever since, draining the life-blood of Ireland to fill the veins of England, and all that makes a nation great and strong and self-respecting was annihilated.

With splendid eloquence the great orators, Grattan, Plunkett, Bushe, denounced the evils of the Union, and their burning words have fed the flame of disaffection to it ever since, but with little result. Concessions, indeed, were made at last, but they came tardily and grudgingly. It is only within a few years that Catholics have been admitted to social and political equality with Protestants- the Catholics of today are the children of the bond-slaves of yesterday; they were born in fetters, and the concessions of England, as they generally do, came too late for gratitude from the embittered hearts of a long oppressed people. But the Irish themselves are also much to blame, their efforts are never organized with the strength and unanimity that produce great results. Religious animosity is the upas tree perpetually distilling its fatal poison upon every broad and liberal project of national advancement. The great French Revolution overthrew the feudal tyranny of a thousand years. Freedom was purchased with much blood, still it was gained; but Irish revolt against oppression only strengthened the fetters; the love of liberty that originated the movement soon degenerated into a rabid hatred of race and creed, and no good fruit has ever grown upon that evil tree.

Other nations have had their seven years' war, or thirty years' war, but Ireland has carried on an utterly unavailing war of seven hundred years, and even yet scarcely recognizes the truth that to raise Ireland to the splendid position in the Empire to which she is entitled, there should be a clear, dignified program of measures, to which all noble natures could say Amen, and the united action of a whole people to obtain their fulfillment.

Disaffection is not an evil where wrongs exist, it is the lever of progress, but incoherent disaffection only scatters and weakens the energies of a people. This is painfully evident in Ireland at the present time, when a mournful and hopeless stagnation rests upon all things; the professions languish, the nobility are absentees, the commercial classes are merely agents for the English manufacturers; there is no stimulus to work, no career, no rewards for intellect, no wealth to support art or literature; and every young man of education and culture must look abroad for a fair opening for his gifts, and be content to leave Ireland to her destiny as a mere cattle-pen for England, and a co-operative store to sell her surplus goods. The ignorance of English statesmen, also, respecting the needs, the history, and even the existing condition of the people, has been highly prejudicial to the country. No large, liberal measures are ever thought of as a remedy for acknowledged 'disaffection.'

Complaint is answered by a coercion bill, and the only remedial act is to proclaim a district. Lord Beaconsfield, though Prime Minister, never visited Ireland, and knew so little of the country he governed- a country that has been devastated, plundered, and three times confiscated, and reduced by want and famine from eight millions to five millions during the last thirty years- that he imputed all the discontent of the Irish solely to their position beside 'the melancholy ocean.' English statesmen might study with advantage the mode by which the Greeks, the great colonizers of the ancient world, gained the love of all peoples. Like England, the Greeks carried on extensive commerce with many strange nations, but they never sought to exterminate; they humanized.

Their trade swept by many shores, but not to destroy, or burn, or ravage. They opened bazaars, they built temples, they planted corn, and erected factories. If they wanted land they took it, but civilized the people, and drew them up into their own higher civilization; they gave their wine and oil for the corn and flax of the stranger, but still more, the wine and oil of their own richly gifted intellects, and they freely intermarried with the foreign peoples, especially with the Celts, between whom and the Greeks there was ever a strong affinity of nature, temperament, and character.

So they passed on in ceaseless migration, founding states wherever they landed, but leaving every state to be self-governed, though bound to Greece by the strong bonds of love and gratitude. Above all people, the Greeks seem to have been endowed with the gift of personal fascination; the English as a nation have none of it, though capable of splendid acts of individual generosity. The colonists were proud to be called Greek, and felt a pride in the triumphs of the Greek name; but in Ireland the word Sassenach inspired only fear, and dread, and hatred. The English strove to crush the mind of the subject race, knowing that culture is power, but the Greeks gave civilization and refinement, art, science, and philosophy. They conquered by their divine gifts, and the colonists in return glorified Greece by their genius, wherever the Greeks passed they left a trail of light, but England a trail of blood.

England never had a divine idea in the treatment of nationalities, least of all in Ireland. Nothing grand or noble in policy was ever thought of to lift the people to their true height. Self was the only motive power; greed of land, greed of wealth the only aim; the lust of gold everywhere, the love of God nowhere; spoilage and insult the only policy, the result being that no nation has ever been so unsuccessful in gaining the love of subject states as England. It is told of the Emperor Aurelian that having decreed the destruction of the city of Tyana, the philosopher Apollonius appeared to him in a dream and said: "Aurelian, if you would conquer, abstain from the destruction of cities; Aurelian, if you would reign, abstain from the blood of the innocent; Aurelian, if you would be loved, be just and merciful."

It is strange that royal races so seldom seem to understand that their only claim to loyalty is in so far as they promote the good of the people. In the government of a nation there should be one thing steadfast- Right; one thing ever sacred- Truth, one thing ever manifested- Love; but this is a gospel seldom preached by statesmen. The prosperity of a country means to them its commercial value, not the moral elevation of the souls committed to their charge. But no doubt there is also some instinctive antagonism, or deficiency of sympathy between English and Irish nature, to account for the eternal war of races, and religions, and temperaments through so many centuries. The English are half made of iron, like their soil; robust, stern, steadfast in purpose, without illusions, without dreams, without reverence, but in the soft, relaxing air of Ireland, the energies of the people are only stirred fitfully, like the sudden storms of their own mountain lakes. There is no persistent force, and the utter stagnation of life, the absence of all motive to exertion forces the people to live in the past, or the future, rather than energetically in the present.

They are always dreaming that to-morrow will give them all they require, for today gives them nothing. The English, on the contrary, in their full overflowing life of the present, have no time for vain lamentations over the past. What Englishman now cares for the devastation of the Commonwealth, even with its solemn tragedy of a king's death, or for the deadly struggle of Guelph and Stuart? The exports of cotton and the price of corn are more to them than the story of all the dynasties since the Conquest. They never loved any of their kings. They have no popular idol in all their history. No great historic fact has become part of the national life. No lofty aspiration inspires their oratory. They live wholly in the sensuous and the actual. The Irish live on dreams and prayer. Religion and country are the two words round which their lives revolve.

The frame-work, also, is different in which their souls are set. The factory smoke is so thick in England the people cannot see heaven. In their hard industrial life their eyes are never lifted from toil; in their ears is only the rush of the wheels and the stroke of the hammer, and the air they breathe is the poison dust of a world-wide commerce. But the Irish, without manufactures or commerce, or anything to do save tend the cattle for English food, can at least live, as it were, in the visible presence of God, in the free enjoyment of lake and river, and mountain unsullied by the smoke of labor. The world above is a reality to the Irish peasant. No people have more intense faith in the unseen. It is their religious temperament, so childlike in its simplicity and trust, that alone makes their life of privation endurable, and enables them to meet all sorrows, even death itself, with the pathetic fatalism expressed in the phrase so often heard from peasant lips, "It was the will of God."

The round, stolid English head, and pale, cold eyes, denote the nation of practical aims, a people made for commerce and industry; while the small oval head of the Celt, and deep, passionate eyes, denote a people made for religion and art; and, therefore, the greatest mistake ever made by England was the endeavor to force the Reformation on a people like the Irish. Protestantism, without art, or beauty, or ritual, or symbol, or reverence, suited the self-asserting, dogged egotism of the English. The right of private judgment means to them simply that every man is as good a judge as the parson, or better. The stolid parishioner pays the clergyman to do a certain duty, as he pays the doctor and the lawyer, but no sanctity surrounds the Protestant priesthood.

The Reformation was a genuine outcome of Saxon nature; a rude revolt against grace, refinement, the beautiful, and the mystic, a cold appeal to the lowest level of the understanding; not a sublime and unquestioning acceptance of an awful revelation from the lips of a consecrated priesthood.

Both in religion and politics the Irish need the visible symbol. Their ideal must be impersonated in some form they can reverence, worship, and love. What sad Irish mother, with her half-famished children round her in their miserable cabin, could bear with life day by day without the infinite trust in the Divine Mother who, she believes, is watching over and pitying her? What could Protestantism with its hard scholastic dogmas do for such a people? In place of the Divine Mother, the solemn emotional ritual, the mystic symbols of altar and cross, they were offered the abstractions of theology in the Thirty-nine Articles; while, with the blasphemous boast that it was the work of God, their stately and beautiful abbeys were plundered and made desolate, where, not self, but the abnegation of self, was the pure ideal of the high ascetic life, and in their place were set up the bare, bleak, whitewashed parish churches.

The Irish, however, found no comfort in the thirty-nine Articles, and would not enter the parish churches. They preferred to die, and so thousands of them were slaughtered with their priests, and the rest were degraded to pariahs in their own land; still, through all the fires of persecution, they clung to their ancient faith, with a fervor that makes the devotion of the Irish to their creed and priesthood, during the bitter martyrdom of three hundred years, one of the most touching chapters in all human history. But new paths opened through the darkness. God has many agents by which peoples and nations are driven forth to be trained and educated by strong, fresh influences. They seem evil at first, yet it is by such means- war, pestilence, and famine- that the human race has been made to drift on, ever westward, during the last three thousand years. The terrible famine that came upon Ireland was one of these agents of God. A million perished miserably, but a million also of the people emigrated.

The Irish peasant was forced at last to rise up from his tireless hearth and blighted fields, to seek a new home across the ocean. From the dismal death-in-life of his wretched existence, with a frame wasted by hunger, and a soul lying torpid in bonds, he was sent forth to gain wealth, power, freedom, and light by contact with a great people of illimitable energies, who needed his toiling hand in exchange for their gold, to build up the chain of cities from the Atlantic to the Pacific, and to lay the rails that span a continent for the traffic of the world.

What may be the future of the much tried, but ineffaceable Irish race, none can tell. No definite line of action has yet been formed, but a people who are learning, under the teaching of America, the dignity and value of human rights, are not likely to acquiesce tamely in the degraded position Ireland holds in Europe, decay stamped on her cities and her institutions, helpless poverty on her people, who yet own a country larger, richer, and better placed for all the purposes of commerce than half the autonomous States of Europe. The Irish never forget their motherland or give up the hope of national independence; even among the kind hearted Americans they have not eaten of the lotus that makes them forget Ithaca. But the regeneration and re-creation of Ireland will not come through 'Home Rule' as understood by its present supporters and leaders, if, indeed, that hollow fiction is not even now almost extinct. No one can seriously believe that the Irish nobles will ever come back to their ancient palaces, or the Queen take up her residence at

Dublin Castle in a desolated city and a land of poverty, torpor, and universal decadence. 'Home Rule,' with its old feudal distinctions of class and caste, is looked upon with bitter disdain by the advanced party in Irish politics, and it will never be galvanized into life again by any amount of platform platitudes.

A National Convention, with supreme power over all that concerns Ireland, and control of the revenues, to be composed of members elected by universal suffrage, and secured in power for a definite time, is the idea most prominently set forth now by the American Irish. Of course a National Convention without the command of the revenues of the nation would be a cheat and a delusion, for the power to make laws and decree improvements would be of little avail as long as the revenue of Ireland was poured into the treasury of another country.

The new movement will have a larger and more comprehensive aim than the mere 'Repeal of the Union.' The American Irish, with their bolder views, desire to create a new system of things, not merely to resuscitate the old, for it is not from the shriveled rags of effete worn-out ideas that a people can weave the garment of the new age. The new wine must be poured into new bottles; and a higher object even than to increase the material prosperity of a country is to create the moral dignity of a people, to bring the torpid, slumbering energies of Ireland within the influence of the powerful electric forces that everywhere else are stirring humanity into new life.

The influence, however, must come from without; Ireland alone and unaided has never yet accomplished one of these great revolutions such as France, Italy, and England have had, that sweep off at once the accumulated evils of centuries, because Ireland has no firm organization, and therefore no power, only a vague nameless discontent, only a bitter sense of wrong. One thing, however, is certain; there is a stir in men's minds now that is a prophecy of change; the feverish unrest that has driven the young generation of Ireland to America will one day drive them back again all alight with her ideas, and ready to proclaim that in a Republic alone is to be found the true force that emancipates the soul and the life of man. England should have counted the cost before compelling the Irish people to take shelter in the arms of the mighty mother of freedom. Yet there is nothing to alarm in the word 'Republic.' It simply means the Government of common-sense for the common good. Every one is wearied with the old system of things, and all long to throw off the incubus of prejudice, and routine, and fetish worship, and to start afresh on a new career under new condition.

The American Irish are eager to join this worldwide movement, which is straining towards a goal set far beyond all merely local aims, or the progress of one's own race and country. America is the great teacher of the nations, and her lessons will eventually lead the world. In '93 American ideas overthrew the thousand-year-old Monarchy of France, and they will probably overthrow the Monarchies of all Europe in time. The next great movement in Ireland will not be a rising of the peasantry against the police, it will be as a part of the European struggle of the masses against a dominant minority. Lines, like hidden electrical wires, of Republican feeling, traverse unseen the whole soil of Ireland a touch will wake them into action.

What the unknown future may bring, none can predict, but another half-century will witness assuredly a new order of things in society and politics. One can hear already the low murmur of the advancing waves of change, and in the endless mutation of all things, Governments, and peoples, and ideas, even Ireland may hope that change will bring progress. It is given to every nation once to touch the zenith, and perhaps the hour of her advancement draws nigh.

But whether the change will come through the clash of war or the peaceful organization of a great European brotherhood of freedom, none can say. The great world-movers of the future will probably cast down before they build up. The iconoclasts will precede the constructors, and the present time is emphatically iconoclastic. All the old-world opinions, dogmas, traditions of custom and usage, all the cumbrous machinery of old-world life and political systems, have been flung into the crucible of the critics and philosophers; but what the residuum will be when the dross is eliminated, who can say?

We can but read the signs of the times, not strive after vain prophecies. It is important, however, that those who rule the nations should study diligently the tendencies of the age throughout Europe, while to England it is of special importance to study the influences from America that are so powerfully affecting the tone of Irish thought, for Ireland may yet be the battle-ground where the destinies of the Empire will be decided. The American Irish are prepared for any effort, any sacrifice to obtain the autonomy of Ireland- that natural right of self government which, as Mr. Gladstone says, belongs to all peoples. Peril and danger may be in the way, but they accept and brave all consequences.

> "They wait beneath the furnace blast,
> The pangs of transformation;
> Not painlessly doth God recast,
> Or mold anew a nation."

Meanwhile England, all-powerful England, may effect a social revolution peacefully, and without any danger to the integrity of the Empire, if wise and just measures are organized in time for the true advancement and prosperity of Ireland; and the Irish people, in return, will stand faithfully by England in those hours of peril which seem gathering in clouds of darkness upon the horizon, and threatening dangers which only a united Empire can meet and overcome.

CONCERNING IRISH PROVERBS

A vast amount of characteristic popular wisdom has existed for ages among the Irish peasantry, condensed in proverbial sayings that show a subtle insight into motives and conduct, with a deep knowledge of all the varied influences that stir the human heart; but though well worthy of a place in our national literature, these proverbs of the people have remained unknown to the general reader, from the fact of their being hidden away in the obscurity of the original vernacular. This hindrance, however, has now, to a great extent, been removed; for, within the last few decades, several eminent Celtic scholars have taken up the subject, and devoted both time and learning, with patient, loving zeal, to the collection and translation into English of many of those interesting examples of ancient thought- the result being that many hundred Irish proverbs have now been rescued from obscurity and made known to English literature, chiefly through the labors of such distinguished men as John O'Donovan; the Rev. Canon Ulick Burke, of St. Jautath's, Tuam, one of the most learned Irish scholars of the age; and Robert MacAdam, of Belfast, editor of The Ulster Journal of Archaeology, whose attention was more particularly devoted to the proverbs of the North of Ireland.

National proverbs form a kind of synthesis of national character and of the moral tendencies of a race. There may be no written code among the peasantry of morals or manners, yet deeper truths concerning human actions, motives, and tendencies often lie at the base of the popular proverbs, than could be gathered from even the most learned and diffuse essays of the philosopher. Irish proverbs are especially remarkable for their concise and forcible expression of truths concerning life, conduct, and action. The matured wisdom of the centuries is in them, and they bear witness to the acute vision of the ancient seers and Pileas, who could fathom the very depths of the human soul, and reveal the mysteries of life in these strong, enduring maxims of steadfast truth. A keen sense, also, of the sad and bitter realities of human destiny is observable in them- the result of shrewd observation, shadowed by the melancholy of age and experience.

The peasants rarely speak on any subject that touches them deeply without illustrating their opinions by a proverb, uttered with the firm decision of assured conviction. Indeed, the peculiar veneration in which the Irish hold the sacred wisdom of their ancestors has given rise to the saying, "It is impossible to contradict the old word" (the proverb).

The Irish people have always believed that their Kings, Brehons, Ollamhs, and Bards were gifted with singular and peculiar intelligence, and a mystic power of reading the secrets of the heart. Hence the sayings of these great wise men of ancient renown have passed through the mind of the people in each successive generation, and are still forever on their lips as so many sacred maxims, to be accepted, without questioning, as undeniable truths respecting their life, words, and works; for many of these proverbs show, in a marked manner, the still ineffaceable peculiarities of Irish nature- the kindness and sensitiveness of the people, their instinctive sense of the grace of courtesy of manner, their love of distinction, their trust in good luck rather than in work, their eminently social qualities, especially the love of conversation, and the pathetic acceptance of the doom that want and poverty bring on life, "because it is the will of God."

These qualities have been connected with the Irish race throughout all history, and are as true now, in the present time, as they have been in the past. Above a hundred years ago, Lord Macartney, the great Ambassador of England to the East, thus described the native Irish; "They are active in body; bold and daring; patient of cold, hunger, and fatigue; dauntless in danger, and regardless of life when glory is in view; warm in love and friendship, quick in resentment, and implacable in hatred; generous and hospitable beyond all bounds of prudence, credulous, superstitious, and vain; talkative, disputatious, and strongly disposed to turbulence and contest. They are all fond of learning, and are endowed with excellent parts, but are usually more remarkable for liveliness of thought than accuracy of expression."

Many of these national and enduring race characteristics will be found expressed with much force and freedom in the following selections from the terse and acute sayings of ancient Irish wisdom.

Selected Proverbs

True greatness knows gentleness.

When wrathful words arise a closed mouth is soothing.

Have a mouth of ivy and a heart of holly.

A silent mouth is musical.

Associate with the nobles, but be not cold to the poor and lowly.

A short visit is best, and that not too often, even to the house of a friend.

Blind should be the eyes in the abode of another.

Great minds live apart; people may meet, but the mountains and the rocks never.

A man with loud talk makes truth itself seem folly.

Much loquacity brings a man's good sense into disrepute, and by a superfluity of words, truth is obscured.

No rearing, no manners.

Tell not your complaints to him who has no pity.

Neither praise nor dispraise thyself; the well bred are always modest.

It is difficult to soothe the proud.

Every nursling as it is nursed; every web as it is woven.

Without store no friends; without rearing no manners.

A little relationship is better than much friendship.

Gentleness is better than haughtiness.

A constant guest is never welcome.

The peacemaker is never in the way.

Forsake not a friend of many years for the acquaintance of a day.

No heat like that of shame.

No pain like that of refusal.

No sorrow like the loss of friends.

No feast till there is the roast.

No galling trial till one gets married.

Praise youth, and it will advance to success.

Reputation is more enduring than life.

Wine is pleasant, unpleasant the price.

Drinking is the brother of robbery.

Character is better than wealth.

If the head cannot bear the glory of the crown, better be without it.

Face the sun, but turn your back to the storm.

Do your work, and heed not boasting.

Without money fame is dead.

He who is up is extolled; he who is down is trampled on.

Sweet is the voice of the man who has wealth but the voice of the indigent man is harsh- no one heeds him.

How many mourn the want of possessions; yet the strong, the brave, and the rich, all go to the grave at last; like the poor, and the emaciated, and the infant.

God is nigher to us even than the door. God stays long,

but He strikes at last.

Death is the poor man's best physician.

Many a day we shall rest in the clay.

A hound's tooth, a thorn in the hand, and a fool's retort are the three sharpest things of all.

Do not credit the buzzard, nor the raven, nor the word of a woman.

No wickeder being exists than a woman of evil temper.

The lake is not encumbered by the swan; nor the steed by the bridle; nor the sheep by the wool; nor the man by the soul that is in him.

Conversation is the cure for every sorrow. Even contention is better than loneliness.

Bad is a bad servant, but he is better than none.

It is sad to have no friend; sad to have unfortunate children; sad to have only a poor hut; but sadder to have nothing good or bad.

There is nothing malicious but treachery.

Idleness is a fool's desire.

Gold is light with a fool.

A long disease does not tell a lie, it kills at last.

Do not take the thatch from your own roof to buy slates for another man's house.

The tree remains, but not the hand that planted it.

A heavy purse makes a light heart.

Better April showers than the breadth of the ocean in gold.

Never count your crops till June is over.

Autumn days come quickly, like the running of a hound upon the moor.

Send round the glass to the south, from the left to the right hand; all things should front the south.

He that spies is the one that kills.

A meeting in the sunlight is lucky, and a burying in the rain.

Winter comes fast on the lazy.

There are three without rule- a mule, a pig, and a woman.

The beginning of a ship is a board; of a kiln, a stone; of a king's reign, salutation; and the beginning of health is sleep.

Have sense, patience, and self-restraint, and no mischief will come.

Four things to be hated: A worthless hound, a slow horse,

a chief without wisdom, a wife without children.

Better a good run than a long standing.

Falling is easier than rising.

One morsel of a rabbit is worth two of a cat.

Cleverness is better than strength.

Good fortune often abides with a fool.

If I am yellow, I have a fair heart.

If the day is long, night comes at last.

Whether the sun rise late or early, the day is as God pleases.

There is no joy without affliction.

No one seeks relationship to the unfortunate.

A foot at rest meets nothing.

The day of storm is not the day for thatching.

Virtue is everlasting wealth.

Avarice is the foundation of every evil.

Wisdom excels all riches.

Shun a prying thief and a deceiver.

An empty vessel has the greatest sound.

Three good things are often thrown away: A good thing done for an old man, for an ill-natured man, or for a child; for the old man dies, the other is false, and the child forgets.

In slender currents comes good luck; in rolling torrents comes misfortune.

Misfortune follows fortune inch by inch.

God never closed one gap but He opened another.

Good begets goodness, and bad badness. Money begets money, and wealth friendship.

Gentleness is better than haughtiness; adjustment than going to law. A small house and full store, than a large house and little food.

Better to spare in time than out of time.

The son of a widow who has plenty of cattle, the foal of an old mare at grass, and the miller's dog who has always plenty of meal, are the three happiest creatures living.

Good luck is better than early rising.

It is better to be lucky than wise.

Every man has bad luck awaiting him some time or other. But leave the bad luck to the last; perchance it may never come.

Have a kind look for misery, but a frown for an enemy.

A misty winter brings a pleasant spring. A pleasant winter a misty spring. Red in the South means rain and cold. Red in the Bast is a sign of frost. Red in the North rain and wind. Red in the West sunshine and thaw.

You will live during the year, for we were just speaking of you.

There is wisdom in the raven's head.

A poem ought to be well made at first, for there is many a one to spoil it afterwards.

A man may be his own ruin. It is a wedge from itself that splits the oak-tree.

Want, slavery, scarcity of provisions, plagues, battles, conflicts, defeat in battle, inclement weather, rapine, from the unworthiness of a prince do spring. In contradistinction to this statement, the reign of a good prince, it is asserted, brings a blessing on the land. In the time of Cormac-Mac-Art, "The world was delightful and happy, nine nuts grew on each twig, and nine sure twigs on each rod." And in the reign of Cathal-Crovh-dhearg, "The grass was so abundant that it reached above the horns of the cattle, when they lay down to rest in the field."

Mysteries and Usages

The ancient Druids, priests, and magi possessed many wonderful secrets. The priest, by waving of his wand, could throw a person into a deep sleep, and while under the influence of this Druidical operation, the patient could describe what was passing at a distance, and exhibit all the phenomena of clairvoyance as known to the moderns. The magi had also the power of prolonging life, and for this purpose an Irish pearl was swallowed, which rendered the swallower as youthful as when in his prime. The Tuatha-de-Danans possessed this secret, hence the tradition of their long existence secreted in caves, after their defeat by the Milesians. The Druids believed that the moon exercised a powerful influence over the human frame, and produced a violent pulsation in the blood-vessels during the space of twenty-four hours. It is reported that the ancient Irish used poisoned weapons, and the poison was extracted from hellebore and the berries of the yew tree. It is believed that if any of the Irish of noble race should die abroad, the dead are so anxious to rest in the ancestral home, that their dust flies on the winds of heaven over land and sea, blasting every green and living thing in its passage as it goes by, until it reaches the hereditary burial ground, and there rests in peace. And this fatal and baneful rush of the dust of the dead, which blights the crops and the fruit, is called by the people, 'The red wind of the hills,' and is held by them in the utmost dread. In the time of the Fenian Princes, the dead were not burned but interred in the earth, the feet to the east, the head to the west; and a cairn of stones was raised over them. Through this, a passage with doors led to the place where the dead lay. A grave of one door for a man of science; a grave of two doors for a woman; mounds over foreigners of distinction; and enclosures round those who died of the deadly plague. Thus, sex and rank were distinguished by the construction of the grave. There was also another mode of burial for warriors. The dead were placed in a standing position, their arms and shield beside them, and a great circular cairn of earth and stones was raised over them. Thus the heroic King of Munster, slain in battle, was placed in his grave. "Mogha-Neid lies in his sepulcher, with his javelin by his shoulder, with his club which was strong in battle, with his helmet, with his sword; long shall he be lamented with deep love, and his absence be the cause of darkest sorrow."

THE END